PIT HEADS
AND
POT BANKS

To Margaret with best wishes

Pauline

PAULINE DAWSON
(DAS-GUPTA)

Published in Great Britain in 2009 by
" Artloaf"
36, The Oval,
Stafford, ST17 4LQ.

ISBN No: 978-0-9546368-1-4.

A catalogue record of this book is available from the British Library.

All photographs are from the authors collection.

Cover from an original watercolour by the author.

Printed by Keele University Graphic Services, Bookbinding and Printing Department.

This book is dedicated to my lovely children,
Anita and John.
For your love and support.
My wonderful grandchildren
Jourdaine, Tilly-Rose,
Jacob, Amy and Elliot.
For your faith and encouragement.

ACKNOWLEDGMENTS.

My thanks to Cerebral Palsy Mid Staff's, Especially to Linda, Janice and Shirley for helping me to navigate my way around a computer. Any profit from the sale of this book will be donated to the above charity.

To Jim Wheeler, "Artloaf"
For his time, invaluable help and advice.

To Gareth Holland,
Keele University Graphic Services,
for his invaluable help and advice.

About The Author.

Pauline Dawson was born in Stoke-on-Trent and raised in Fenton. The oldest of seven children, born to parents from a working class background. Father a bricklayer, was always in full time employment, and in great demand on the side during evenings and weekends. Mother was a stay at home mum, child rearing over a number of years. Pauline was educated in state schools in Fenton, followed by a pre-nursing course at the Elms Technical College. General nurse training at the North Staff's Royal Infirmary, followed by midwifery training at the City General Hospital and The Limes. In the 1960's she married a doctor from the Indian subcontinent, who's medical training took them to various parts of the country including areas of Staffordshire. In 1967 they settled in Stafford where they still live.

CONTENTS.

THE GOOD OLD DAYS.

There's money in pots and pits, they'd say. It was true, but not for the poor folks that worked in them. The early part of the twentieth century had been bad. The first world war, left widows and orphans galore. The depression in the twenty's wasn't much better. The skinny, pale faces that marched from Jarrow, would almost be mirrored by the returning prisoners of war, a couple of decades later.

Until the second world war, many died of consumption, tuberculosis was it's proper name. It was the cancer of the time and true, some poor people that escaped the consumption, would die of starvation. It was an England of soup kitchens and national assistance, a pittance, doled out to anyone who hadn't two half pennies to rub together. Even under these circumstances, there was still the British stiff upper lip and some would rather starve, than sell their souls, as they'd say, a very proud race in those days.

What people lacked in money, they had in camaraderie. Everybody was in the same boat, but, there was support and sharing, neighbourhoods were communities and they survived by helping each other. The potteries grew from such communities. Generations of the same families, lived next door, the same row, the next street, the same town. Rows of terraced houses, built around pot banks and pit heads. The working classes, didn't own cars in those days, so it was necessary, to live in close proximity to one's place of work.

It wasn't unknown, for there to be serious accidents either, especially in the pits. Most of the owners were only concerned for their bank balances. The people that created their wealth, were of little or no consequence. At times like this, the true spirit of neighbours was seen at the pit heads, as they stood, side by side, kids tugging at their skirts as they waited for news, hoping for the best but dreading the worst.

The ones down the pits, were the ones that hadn't gone off to war. Ten percent of the male work force, were conscripted to work in the pits. The Bevan boys as they were called. They were the ones left behind, to dig out the coal with picks and shovels. Digging through the coal face, shoring up the roof, often no more than three feet above their heads, as they struggled on their bellies. It was their job, to keep the rest of us warm, keep the power stations and gas plants going. The gas and electricity that we had then, was produced by burning coal. Natural gas had never been heard of and the only use for nuclear energy, was in Inola Gay, the bomb, used to obliterate Hiroshima on the sixth of August 1945. Pit head baths were provided for the miners returning from the pit face, but a familiar sight was a group of miners, black faces, white eyes and white teeth. A lot of these men ended up with dust disease, Pneumoconiosis. While the men worked in the pits, the women, apart from the aged and those in poor health, were working in the ammunitions factories at Swynnerton and other places around North Staffordshire. Many young, single women worked on the land and across the country were conscripted, put in uniform and farmed out as it were. This became known as the land army.

In their spare time, especially at night, the men left at home became involved in the ARP or air raid patrol.The Germans were fond of our area, due to the munitions factories and the railway systems, used for transporting equipment and supplies. One such fellow lived next door to us. We would get a knock on the door and it was up, out of our comfortable beds and down to the Anderson shelter, there were also Morrison shelters. Every family had a shelter, usually situated in the back garden or yard. They were issued and erected, by the councils, at the start of the war. The schools also had air raid shelters, as I was later to find out. In our shelter we kept pillows, blankets and a few other essentials, a raid, could go on all night, so it was better to be prepared. One of the most important things was the wooden boxes, containing our gas masks, we were never without these. It was pitch black, we weren't even allowed a candle and if anyone took the risk, there would be a huge blast, from the wardens silver whistle. The gas lamps in the streets remained unlit. The air raid wardens patrolled their area from dusk to dawn, checking that not a chink of light could be seen through the windows, the panes taped up, to stop the glass shattering in the event of an explosion. The german bombers had an unmistakable drone. The distance or proximity to us was measured by this terrifying sound. When the siren finally sounded the all clear, we could go back in doors and hopefully to bed. There was no guarantee that we would not be up again later in the night.We kept our shelter long after the war and used it to play in, especially when the weather was bad. It wasn't warm in there, but at least it was dry.

The war was a time of rationing, especially food and textiles. Everybody was issued with ration books, containing coupons which were removed when a purchase was made. I was registered as a vegetarian, which allowed my mother extra eggs, cheese, butter and milk, these were cheaper than meat and, I guess she could make more use of them. Vegetables were plentiful, everybody had a vegetable plot. Terraced houses had small back yards, no such thing as a manicured lawn and pretty flowers. Often a path of Staffordshire blue brick, which led from the back door to the coal house and outside toilet at the bottom of the yard. In some cases, a zinc bath would be

The Good Old Days.

hanging on the wall, brought inside once a week, for family bath time. A family would be self sufficient in home grown vegetables and anything to spare would be given to a bigger family or senior citizen. There were no freezers, so it couldn't easily be stored. Local councils allocated plots of land to local citizens for such cultivation. The allotments as they were called, many still in use in the twenty first century. These people would sell their produce in the local markets and it was there, that we would buy any extras. We were canny shoppers, it was said, if it doesn't have dirt on it, it isn't fresh, so we knew what to look out for.

The cessation of hostilities in Europe, couldn't come soon enough and when announced, was received with much relief. Everyone, started saving their meagre ration coupons in order to throw a few good street parties. Union jacks and bunting, decorated streets from end to end. There were linen covered tressle tables arranged down the length of the road. Council permission didn't need to be sought or granted, neither were permits required to prohibit vehicles, since there weren't very many of those around to worry about. Our street was no different to any others and we duly had our big bash. I went to our party in an outfit made out of union jacks, mum was handy with a sewing machine. Infact, most women were, it was a necessity. The day of these parties, was the one day when everybody got stuck in. Nothing was spared, most people kept a few tins in the pantry, for rainy days or special occasions. It all appeared at once and we all left stuffed.

Servicemen started to return, a trickle at first and we waited with baited breath. There were kids who would never see their dad again. My brother and I were lucky, our dad came back. I don't remember, whether, I was more interested in him or his huge kit bag, I couldn't empty it quick enough. My dad had been a dispatch rider in north Africa, so our small gifts were typical of that region. I shall never forget, my lovely little decorated, light leather handbag and a wooden giraffe, made of individual different coloured woods, it was very realistic, even the ears were shaped from wood. They became treasured possessions for a number of years. As part of the demobilisation package, servicemen were given a voucher to exchange for an outfit which helped them get back into civilian life. It was often called a demob suit. The voucher could be exchanged at a well known high street tailor called Montague Burton. The package consisted of a suit, shirt, tie and a pair of shoes. If a good deal was struck a trilby was included, in this case, it was said that the guy had the "full monty".

There were a few, American army camps around our area and it wasn't unknown, for the locals to cavort with the G.I's the name given to the American personnel, many of them would be in the local dance halls, ending up in the alleyways after they'd pulled. Needless to say, some of our returning troops, found they had kids, they didn't remember, leaving

behind. Strangely enough, on the whole, the situation seemed to be accepted. Maybe, men in those days, only understood certain parts of the reproductive process, the bit that gave them the most pleasure. After all, there was no sex education classes in schools then. I know for a certain fact, that after my birth, I was the first of seven, my father expected my mother to have an abdominal scar. He actually didn't know how babies came out. He certainly knew how they got in, or did he? No doubt, there were more than a few, pale faced sprogs left around Europe and north Africa. When the future is so uncertain, caution is thrown to the wind. I guess it was a case of, what's source for the goose is source for the gander. Lips were sealed and thoughts kept secret.

Rationing continued for several years, until it was finally abolished in 1954. By this time, the situation had been getting easier, but, for many a year, we had known poor food and little of it.We had also got used to the cold, inside and out. The whole house would be heated by one coal fire. The warmest bedroom, if there was such a place, was the one with the chimney breast running through it. Behind the fire was a back boiler, which provided hot water. It is hard now to imagine the bone penetrating chill, that pervaded the whole place. On waking, in the mornings, it wasn't uncommon, to see your own breath in the bedroom. The floors were covered in linoleum or lino as it was generally called, a peg rug might be beside the bed, to take the chill off the feet as the bed covers were reluctantly removed. I remember getting out of bed and stuffing my clothes, underneath the bed covers to warm up, before putting them on. In fact, in order to keep warm at night, we wore a number of layers, we often said, that we got undressed, only to get dressed again.

Our fire would be made up of a couple of large pieces of black shiny coal, once this got hot, slack, a type of powdered coal, would be poured at the back, using a small hand shovel. This procedure made the coal last a lot longer. The winters seemed colder then, it is no joke, but we actually had jack frost or ice crystals, on the inside of our windows. A couple of our bedrooms which happened to be the biggest of the three, had small cast iron fireplaces. When it was really bad, dad would dig a shovel of hot coals from the main fireplace, carry them upstairs and put them in the bedroom fire grate, it took the chill off the room. My brother and I would take turns to stay awake and keep an eye on the fire, making sure that it didn't catch the bed covers. I'm sure that we didn't keep this up for long, but the intention was sincere enough. The windows weren't the only thing to freeze on the inside. There were times, when nothing would come out of the tap. A saucepan of water was kept on the gas cooker overnight, it too, would be frozen by morning. The gas would be ignited and as the ice melted, we had water! this was boiled and used to pour over the tap and pipes to thaw them out. I don't remember having many burst pipes, but dad soon fixed them, they were made of lead in those days.

The outside toilet could be a nightmare, unlit and unheated. Our dustbin was metal, possibly zinc, the lid would be put on the concrete floor of the toilet, bowl side upwards. Dad would carry a shovel full of hot coals and fill the bin lid, in the hope that it would prevent the cistern and toilet bowl from freezing. It wasn't always effective. You knew about that if you were the first to have a pee in the morning and you heard the ice cracking in the pan. That was after gingerly sitting on the freezing bakelite seat, wood was a little warmer, but choice didn't exist.

The fuel for this extra heating didn't always come via the coalman, who arrived down the backs, driving a flat topped truck, loaded with sacks of coal, each weighing one hundredweight. He would stand, with his back to the truck, hands over his shoulders and lift the sack. It was then carried, on his back and tipped over his head into the appropriate place. Not, always appropriate, our coalhouse, as they were called was a small room off our kitchen. When the coal was tipped, the black dust it threw up was wicked. One day, I was sitting at the table, enjoying a slice of bread and butter and an orange, when the coalman left, it was covered in coal dust and inedible, end of my tea, that day. My grandma's house had a cellar and the coal was tipped down there through a vent in the front garden. More than once I heard my grandma say " make sure there's plenty of lumps, we're not paying for a bag of slack", and she would go down the cellar and check, before she paid. One bag, was all anybody had in a week, nobody could afford anymore. During the summer, the stock built up, which meant that we had a bigger supply, for the winter, though, there were times when this wasn't enough.

One winter springs readily to mind and must have been one of the worst on record, it was 1947. Slag heaps became more useful than ever, as did wheels. Anything that had two wheels was put into service, four wheels even better. Bicycles of whatever age, had a box strapped to the back of the seat, bags, would be hung over the back wheel like panniers and as many bags as possible, would be hung over the handle bars. Old prams and some not so old, even just sets of wheels, which had a piece

of wood laid across the chassis. Whole families and neighbours would trek to the nearest slag heap to pick the coal. The slag heaps were covered in humanity, which appeared from everywhere. Age was no barrier to this job either, if you were able to walk, you were able to pick up a piece of coal and drop it into a bag or box. We were told to pick the bigger, shiny pieces. There were no lumps to be had, but, at that point everything was a bonus and
hopefully kept the fire going. This particular winter, seemed to last forever and the trek to the coal tip as it was often called, became a regular event, almost a social gathering. Inspite of such hardship, people managed and there was always a helping hand for those unable to make the trek.

Things became very different in the second half of the twentieth century. Identity cards were abolished, soon after ration cards, supposedly, in order to enhance personal freedom. I still have mine, kept for posterity. Thinking about the argument for and against identity cards in the twenty first century and the changes in our society, perhaps, it would have been better had they been retained.

CHANGING ROOMS.

Home textiles, fabrics and ready made clothes were rationed well into the fifties. Recycling today, is nothing in comparison to the days of rationing. Clothes were passed up, passed down and even passed sideways. Sometimes you wouldn't know who the clothes on your back belonged to.

Woollens, when they became thick due to washing, would be unpicked, unravelled, wound into balls and re knit into a smaller garment. This process could happen more than once and, probably, something that was once Dad's sweater, ended up as a pair of socks. Even these would often get darned when the heel or toes wore out. There was no nylon to reinforce and every female was adept at darning.

Shirt tails were cut off and used to repair parts of the shirt that had worn, like the collar and cuffs. God knows what some of the men did for wiping their backsides, when they lost their tails. Talk about skid marks, it was a mega slide after a week.

When double bed sheets became worn, that's to say threadbare, the middle strip was cut out. The two good halves sewn together to make a single sheet, sleeping on the join could be pretty uncomfortable. The recycling went on, a single sheet would become pillow cases or cot sheets. Plenty of these were used because there were some really big families then and that's where changing rooms came in. It's not a new invention but, there's a big difference. Now, it means new décor, new textiles, even new silk flowers and twigs to match. Then, it was changing the rooms to suit the needs of the family.

The larger number of children of the same sex had the bigger room and there could be as many as three beds to a room. More often than not, there was more than one kid to a bed. Bunk beds weren't invented, so it was top to toe, two at the top, one at the bottom. If one kid wet the bed, everyone would be saturated and stink of pee and that, on only one bath a week, phew!! Mostly parents would have the smaller room, which would about accommodate a double bed and the obligatory cot.Now, you'd think that would be the end of a well used cot sheet, far from it. It would be cut into strips, which would be folded, loops stitched to either end and hey presto, it became a sanitary towel which, would be washed and re used as and when necessary.

Curtains could be dyed and re used. If they'd served their time, they were often made into a dress or skirt. Any odd pieces of fabric or clothes which couldn't be found a better use, would be cut into small strips, approximately 1inch x 4inch and stored for later use, by which I mean the making of a peg rug. Potatoes, onions and sprouts etc,weredelivered to greengrocers in hesian sacks. These were in great demand and anyone would do whatever necessary to get hold of any that may be available. We would often perform tasks such as sweeping out the shop, which had wooden floor boards and would be really dusty from potato soil and onion skins. Another job would be delivering customers orders to their homes. This was a common practice, there were several small grocery and greengrocery shops, customers always had what they called, order books. The order books were filled out with requests for goods such as, butter 8oz, sugar 1lb, cheese 6oz and so on. Normally one of the kids would deliver the order book to the appropriate shop. The shop would put up the order and it would be delivered, often by bicycle, to the customer. The shops were always on the look out for delivery boys and girls. The reward, besides a few coppers, were hesian sacks, as many as you could get your hands on.

The sacks would be unstitched and sewn together again, according to the required size of the rug. A pattern would be drawn on the hesian, the strips of fabric, colour sorted and the job of pegging would begin using a special tool. Often two or three would be working on the rug at the same time. The only place you see these relics now are in working museums,

Changing Rooms.

depicting life in the nineteenth and twentieth
centuries. The peg rug was the predecessor of
the more up market ready cut rug, a company
that did very well for quite a number of years,
as many young women took it up as a hobby.
It declined as other hobbies took over and
fashions changed.

Nothing was thrown away, a use was normally
found for everything. Even the ashes, left over
from the coal fire, would be used on the ice in
winter, to prevent anyone slipping. Newspaper
was cut into squares, threaded onto a piece of
string, then hung on a nail in the outside
lavatory. We didn't get to read the news from
our backsides either, the print didn't come off
then like it does now. Other newspaper, was
taken to the local fish and chip shop. There, it
would be exchanged for a bag of fish bits. We'd
fair make a meal of these, a good dollop of salt
and vinegar, bread and butter if we were lucky.
Actually there was no fish, they were just
pieces of fried batter. We would collect
newspapers from older neighbours, who's
children had grown up, and take them to the
chippy, in the sure knowledge that a tasty
treat would be forthcoming.

Every so often, the rag and bone man came, he
got his name from what he collected, though
up to this day, I don't know where he got the
bones from. He would drive an old cart, pulled
by a poor bedraggled horse, down the backs, a

sort of service road which ran behind the back gardens of two rows of houses. I guess the rags he collected would be sold for paper making. I don't know what he did with the bones, if he ever got any. The contributors to his collection never got paid, but, the kids would get something like a balloon. Anything from the rag and bone man would be a treat to us. As soon as we heard his cry, "rag and bone, rag and bone", we'd run in and beg for some rags, so that we'd get whatever treat was on offer. Whatever we gave him had absolutely no other use and had come to the end of the road. On one occasion he was giving out one day old chicks. It seems anything went back then and it's not all that long ago. He would be taken to court for cruelty now and rightly so. However, we were given two or three, whether we gave him lots of rags, or, whether he just wanted to get rid of the chicks is in doubt. The chicks were duly placed in a shoe box and kept in the top oven of the range, the door remained open, to avoid them being cooked alive. I suppose, it was a sort of makeshift incubator. We gave them water and bread. We were totally ignorant of their welfare, but set out to rear them, no doubt for dinner at a later date. I have to report, that sadly they died within two days.

In most houses the curtains, especially the ones on the front windows, all matched. The colour didn't necessarily match the décor of the rooms, just so long as it looked uniform from the outside. On the whole they weren't lined, ration coupons didn't stretch to lining, and, as a kid I wouldn't have known what a lined curtain looked like. A school trip once took me to London and a look at Buckingham Palace. I surprised everybody back home, by telling them, that Buckingham Palace had sheets up to the windows, and they all believed me!! The curtains in our house were attached to hooks which had small metal wheels at one end. These were fitted to a metal track, along which the wheels would run, when the curtains were opened and closed. The metal tracks were hidden by a valance, often referred to as a frill. It had more of a practical use, than a decorative idea which it later became.

Soft furnishings didn't match, whatever was available and more importantly, affordable, were the determining factors as to colour, fabric type and shape. Table cloths, towels and bed sheets were always white, mostly cotton but, very occasionally linen because it was more expensive. Woollen blankets were used on the beds. They were washed every year, but, never before the end of May. There was an old wives saying, "wash your blankets before May, wash your family away". With washing, they became thicker until eventually, they were so small, they hardly tucked in. It was quite posh to have the bed covered with a cotton counterpayne. What would our

Changing Rooms.

grandmothers think of all the scatter cushions
that now cover the beds during the day, only to
end up on the floor overnight.

MAKING ENDS MEET.

It is said, that if you keep it long enough, it will come back into fashion, as a general rule that is true. However, up until the fifties, women and housewives in particular wore the same thing day in day out. It was almost regulation uniform and consisted of several items. The turban was universal, a square headscarf, folded into a triangle. This was placed over the head with the apex over the forehead. The other two ends would be brought around the base of the head and tied in a knot over the apex, which would then be pulled over the knot and tucked in. The turban usually covered Dinky metal curlers, these would be in all week and only removed either, on Saturday night for the weekly dance, at the Kings hall in Stoke or the Queens in Burslem or on Sunday for church.

The second component of the outfit would be a wrap over pinafore, always made of cotton and usually covered in a small floral print. The pinafore covered whatever tatty clothes were worn underneath. On their feet would be well worn shoes, sandals or slippers often referred to as trashers. Not only was this outfit worn around the house and garden, it is what most women wore to work on the potbanks. Ladies of a higher social standing were more suitably attired and would wear a nice starched white apron often trimmed with fine lace. This was used to protect their finer clothes as opposed to hiding tattered garments.

Making Ends Meet.

As kids we wore a liberty bodice, a white, fairly thick cotton garment that covered our chest area, it was almost a waist coat. It fastened down the front with small rubberised buttons. As we got older, it would be boned, in order to make us sit up straight. Some had suspenders that were used to hold up our thick blue or brown stockings. Once we started school, we wore navy blue knickers which had elastic around the legs as well as the waist. There was a little pocket on the right hand side for a handkerchief, if you were lucky, otherwise you were one of the regular snotty nosed kids with a rather stiff jumper sleeve. These knickers would be a turn off for anybody and had the very apt name of chastity draws.Uniform wasn't worn in our day, except for those attending the high school or grammar school. We wore whatever was available, a motley looking crew at times I guess. As children, dressing and undressing would be done in the living room, in front of the fire, most of the clothes being dumped on the floor until they were folded and put in piles ready for the next day.

Once a year we were all kitted out, head to toe with a new outfit, usually, for the occasion of the annual Sunday school anniversary, so we were some of the best dressed kids on the stage. There was never any money left over from the house keeping allowance. A weekly amount that the man of the house handed over from his pay packet, the rest was his and nobody ever knew exactly how much that was. This practice was wide spread and the house keeping pittance, not only fed and clothed the family but, paid the rent, collected weekly by the rent man, an employee of the council. The amount paid was recorded in his book and also in the book that was kept by the tenant. Coins also had to be fed into the gas and electric meters otherwise, the lights went out. The meters were emptied by the gas or electric man, as they were referred to. The cost for the amount used was taken and any amount left over would either be fed back into the meter or handed over and used as a bonus. Coal, delivered by the hundred weight and the window cleaner all expected and got a cash payment. Wages were paid in cash, usually in a little brown envelope which also contained a payslip; Joe public didn't have a bank account in those days. The only other callers were the milkman; every house had a daily delivery. The insurance man, usually from the Prudential always shortened to the man from the Pru. As kids were born, a life insurance would be taken out at the cost of a penny a week, called a penny policy.

To kit a large family out all in one go wasn't easy and to make ends meet the Provident cheque came into its own. It was in effect a loan in the form of a cheque. It would be presented at the shop in payment. The amount spent would be deducted and the remaining balance calculated, this procedure continued until it was all spent. It was paid back on a weekly basis with interest. The provident man would call on a Friday night when he could guarantee getting paid because it was pay day. He had a regular round; it was his main occupation, so the provident cheque was in great demand, in a way, helping to spread the cost.

The clothes bought on this occasion would be our Sunday best and would be kept pristine, as they would serve that purpose for the next twelve months. A practice that has stayed with many to this day, including me. I find difficulty in wearing so called best clothes on a daily basis, new clothes are kept for special occasions. It is both irritating and infuriating to discard best clothes, either because they become too big, too small or just unfashionable.

The turbans and pinafores, worn six days a week by the working class, who formed the majority, would be replaced by best on Sunday for church or Saturday night for the dance halls. On these occasions especially on Saturday night, the men would be smartly dressed, out to impress, often in a suit with turn up trousers, shirt and tie. If they really wanted to pull, which was after all the aim of most, a white silk scarf with a fringe was worn loosely around the neck, there might be only one scarf in a family and whoever got dressed first, got the scarf. These fella's were nicknamed spivs, real show off's.Jeans hadn't been invented and there was no such thing as casual wear. It was either working clothes or best.

During and after the war, the only available hosiery for women were silk stockings. These were expensive and used up too many coupons. There were a fair number of G.I's billeted around the towns; it was not unusual for them to frequent the local dance halls and pubs. It could be possible to get a pair from a local G.I.possibly in return for a favour or two, and anyone wearing them were at risk of being labelled a loose woman. Stockings were held up by suspender belts or for the slightly heavier woman, corsets. The suspenders had rubberised studs which, had a habit of perishing and breaking off. Any number of items would be used in place of a broken stud, necessity being the mother of invention, a small button or a small coin if one was available. It wasn't unknown for an aspirin to be put to such use and when it was, a date would often feign a headache. In the absence of stockings the legs were stained, often with gravy browning. An eyebrow pencil was used to draw a line, hopefully straight, up the back of the leg to represent a stocking seem. A rain shower would cause problems and striped legs would result. When women dressed up, especially for church on Sunday the outfit was considered incomplete without a hat. It didn't do to overdress or to be seen to be wearing something that might look a little bit expensive. Such people were labelled as all fur coat and no knickers. In other words all top show, nothing of substance underneath. On dance nights it didn't do to show too much flesh, women were expected to be decent even on these occasions, otherwise they risked being compared to a gangsters moll.

Make up was limited to Max Factor pan stick foundation. It was actually a stick of solid foundation. It was rubbed on the face and then evened out with a damp sponge. Loose powder was applied with a puff, rouge highlighted the cheek bones. Mascara was used for the eye lashes. The mascara came in block form in a plastic compact which also had a small application brush. The mascara was rendered useable by the addition of saliva. The small brush would be held to the lips, where, it would be spit upon, this would then be rubbed onto the mascara block and then applied to the eye lashes. Lipstick was generally used; the colours available were pretty basic and mostly red. Make up was never allowed in our house, it was considered worldly to adorn oneself. I called at my grandmother's house one night, when I was either, old enough to decide for myself or brave enough to face the wrath of my mother. I was wearing the reddest of red lipstick. On seeing me, my grandmother exclaimed "good god, you look as though you've fallen down the cellar steps and caught your mouth on a nail", a great confidence boost.

Perfume was used very sparingly, sometimes begged and sometimes borrowed, it was a treat and only used on very special occasions. There wasn't a vast array, but the most popular of the day was Evening in Paris, this came in a small navy blue bottle which had a small silver screw top. I always begged my aunts used bottle, no matter how empty, I would manage to squeeze a few drops for something special. The other one that springs to mind was White Fire. This came in a very small red bottle with a small golden screw top which had a twist, sort of representing a flame. Eau de Cologne as in 4711 or Yardley's Old English Lavender were considered poor substitutes to us young ones. If you were really, really poor and found soap and water insufficient, after all, they were mainly applied once a week then you could always fall back on phul nana.

The most popular dances of the day were, the jive and the jitterbug, a dance imported from America by the G.I.'s. They were both very energetic dances and were replaced in the fifties and sixties by rock and roll from Bill

Making Ends Meet.

Haley's rock around the clock and the twist. These dances didn't manage to outlive the old ballroom favourites such as the waltz, quickstep and foxtrot etc.

Women would never be seen in trousers which didn't really become part of the female wardrobe until the seventies. Skirt lengths varied throughout the twentieth century as much as they do now. Early in the century, skirts were long, it was considered modest for a woman to cover her legs. Just after the Second World War, skirts were straight and were just above knee length. The reason for this change was a shortage of fabric and rationing, the fact that showing a leg was one way of attracting the opposite sex, was definitely not on the agenda ha! ha! These skirts were worn with high heeled shoes, often with a peep toe. Platforms and wedge heel were fashionable and some were really classy. They came around again in the seventies and are back again in the twenty first century. If only I'd kept the odd pair or two. As the restrictions on fabric were eased, skirts became fuller infact circular in the fifties. Three or four net petticoats would be worn underneath to fill them out. They were worn with well cut blouses.

In the late fifties and sixties, the mini skirt made an appearance; it was the start of a new fashion era and raised more than a few eyebrows. As the wearers became bolder, the skirts became shorter and the micro mini came on the scene. It was referred to as a rather wide belt rather than a very short skirt. At about the same time another new fashion hit the high street, in the form of very short shorts. These were referred to as hot pants. They were so short; they were almost a mini skirt with a crotch, perhaps giving a little respectability to the very short skirts. We always had winter coats, inspite of the description; they were our only coat and were worn all year round. They were probably the most expensive item in the wardrobe, it was purchased with plenty of room and length to spare, in the hope that it would last at least two, possibly three years and more than likely passed down after that.

Hair styles changed according to the fashion of the day. Men always had a parting and the hair was heavily brillcreemed with a quaff at the front. In the thirties and forties women had a centre parting with a sweep on either side. A small side comb would sweep the hair back from the temple area and the comb would be pushed back into the hair to secure the style. The longer hair was formed into a roll, using a fabric thread or ribbon, around which the hair was rolled. The ends being secured by grips hidden in the side sweeps. The page boy was popular, the hair rolled under rather than over and finished with a matching fringe. Ringlets were common for school girls; this was achieved by wrapping the hair in rags overnight. When curls were the fashion of the day, women would go to extraordinary lengths, often employing very uncomfortable means to achieve a good result. These included waving tongues and curling tongues which had to be heated, usually by being put in the coal fire for a few minutes. As people became better off hair was curled using a semi permanent hair perm often done at home. The results were always unpredictable, a bit of hit and miss. Hair could be curled; however, it could not be straightened. It could also be dyed and there were the proverbial bottle blondes, achieved by the use of peroxide, bought by the bottle from the chemist. None of these treatments were very good for the hair and remedies suggested to counteract the damage, included such things as egg yolk and vinegar. In the fifties there was a proliferation of hairdressers as shorter styles became more fashionable. Early teenagers were queuing to get the Urchin cut and the D.A. short for ducks arse, so called because each side was brushed back, to meet in a line at the centre of the back of the head, resembling the feathered anatomy of the duck. With these styles came the desperate need to carry a comb. In the evenings, we would hang around lamp posts, constantly combing our hair. If we became a nuisance, we were told to move on to the front of our own houses.

Making Ends Meet.

Over the last sixty years, fashions have not so much changed as been rehashed. From turn ups, straight leg and flares, single and double breasted. Open toe, closed toe, wedges, high heels or flatties. Skirt lengths have constantly fluctuated from the ankle to the gluteal fold. Where do all the fashion designers get their ideas from? What's new? Basically, not a lot.

A PROPER PARTY.

Though many foods were scarce and, there were times in the twenty's, thirty's and forty's, when some members of our society could barely afford the basics. One of the reasons for the Jarrow march, starvation. This aside, in the forty's and fifty's we generally had full belly's. The contents of our stomachs would no doubt raise a few eyebrows today, the age of five portions of fruit and veg a day, little red meat and few carbohydrates. How did so many of our forebears live to the ripe old age of 85 and 90 years? Of course, life was much different then; a much more active lifestyle was employed. Meat was locally reared and properly fed; antibiotics and fattening agents weren't used as they are now. Vegetables were always available, as most people grew their own, either in their small back yards or in allotments rented from the council. The allotment holders also sold their produce for a small return. Fruit was quite different, because we only had what would grow in our northern hemisphere climate and for that reason it was seasonal. Imported food was quite uncommon. Transportation was limited, there were no refrigerated container trucks plying the continent as now and air transport was new and very costly.

We had ways and means of storing for the winter, what we grew in the summer. Apples were stored individually, in straw and kept in a cool place, they were also specific to our

A Proper Party.

country, i.e. Cox's Orange Pippin and Worcester. The Vale of Evesham, was then as now, known for the growing of fruit. That area became the centre for cider making, for obvious reasons.

When the fruit was ready for harvesting, groups of young people, sometimes whole families would move to these areas for work. They would be given food and accommodation would be provided in and around the farms and orchards. It was in many cases considered the family holiday. At the end of the day, groups would gather, the kids could run around, well away from danger while their parents enjoyed a jar of cider or ale, crack a few jokes and have a little sing song before turning in for the night, a type of gypsy lifestyle for a couple of weeks. A far cry from today, when we are having to employ immigrant workers to do the job, the mobile homes used to house them, can be seen around many of our farms. Picking and handling fruit is not compatible with machinery and so is labour intensive.

Oranges were about the only thing I can remember being imported, usually from Spain. Grapes did grow in England but, not on a big scale. The reason why, for many years, grapes were special and usually taken as a treat only to someone who was sick, so, if you were never sick enough, you never got to taste a grape. Soft fruit was freely available here as in rhubarb, plums, damsons, greengages and pears etc. These were stewed and bottled, using Kilner jars which had a very air tight lid. These would be kept for months, usually for special occasions such as Christmas or a special birthday. According to the amount of sugar available, many soft fruit was made into jam and there was a good variety, strawberry, gooseberry, blackcurrant, plum and damson to name a few. This was stored in jars, usually sealed with greaseproof paper, before the lid was applied. The bottles and jars would be sterilised, by pouring boiling water in them, it was done in a manner so as not to crack the glass. If it was not done properly, the contents would go mouldy, a lot of food and effort gone to waste, it didn't happen very often.

Any tomatoes that did not ripen during the summer, were picked while still green and, either put on a window sill to ripen in whatever sunlight was left, made into a green tomato chutney or stored in a cool dark place for use in the winter. Sauce, ketchup and salad cream wasn't used often due to its cost, but we always had pickles. There would always be jars of pickled shallots, red cabbage and a few jars of mixed pickles which contained cauliflower, cucumber and shallots. Cucumber and onion was always on the table for tea on Sunday. They were both finely sliced and marinated in vinegar. The left overs would be used on bread and butter the next day.

Apart from pickling and bottling, food was not easily stored. Refrigerators were not available to the ordinary household, until well into the sixties. Everyone had a larder or pantry as some were called, mainly depending on the locality. The larder or pantry tended to be a small room off the kitchen. This was where the majority of food was kept. The jars and bottles on shelves. Most pantry's had a slab or still, it was really a piece of concrete with a space above and below. It was generally situated on a north facing wall, as this was always the coolest. In the houses of the rich and famous, this would no doubt have been marble, however it was always cold. Food such as cold meat, cheese and butter were kept on the slab as was milk, usually in a jug, bought by the pint from the churn. Anything that needed to be kept for a few days would be placed on the still or slab. Whatever there was, if anything, wouldn't be on there for very long anyway. What we had was needed and nothing was wasted either.

We always had a roast on Sunday. Whatever meat was left on the bone or joint, would be cut into cubes on Monday and made into lobby, the Staffordshire stew, in our house it was called resurrection dinner a very apt term, throughout the week the food was hashed and rehashed to provide a daily meal. Lobby consisted of everything being thrown into a saucepan, onions, carrots and loads of potatoes; they were not only filling but cheap. It was all bulked up by the addition of pearl barley and, in times of plenty, a few suet dumplings might be thrown in too. On Tuesday, the bone was boiled and a soup was made, this was served up in bowls and chunks of bread were put in to soften or dunked. Any cooked, left over vegetables, would be mashed and fried with a little butter in the frying pan and made into a sort of potato cake, sometimes served hot with cold meat and pickled cabbage. So, the rations were put to good use. The poor meat ration was probably the biggest hardship; it was also the most expensive. Once the ingenuity ingredient was added, the results were phenomenal, and would put most cooks to shame nowadays. Inexpensive meat was used at other times, a regular item was sausage and mash, the sausage actually contained little meat, especially, due to there being no minimum meat requirement in any processed food at that time. Liver and onions was another filler. Though the war ended in 1945, it was to be another nine years before rationing was ended in 1954.

During the period of rationing, the ways and means act was often employed, it was necessary for survival. Puddings were not a regular feature on the menu and often, when they were, they contained foods which today would be put in the bin. Stale bread was used for bread pudding, a real stodge, which filled your belly and kept you warm in winter. It basically consisted of bread, soaked in cold tea, added to which would be some dried fruit and a beaten egg; this was put into a greased dish, sugar sprinkled on top and then cooked in the oven. Occasionally, we had bread and butter pudding, a bit more up market. A big dish of rice pudding was sometimes in the oven, my favourite part was the skin and there would be a fight for the dish, just to scrape the sides. Another favourite filler was suet pudding or spotted dick. We would get a lump of suet, which is basically fat; it would be grated and mixed with other ingredients, rolled in flour and put into a cloth which was tied at both ends. It was then cooked by boiling for what seemed hours and then served with jam or custard. On special occasions or Sundays, we had tinned or bottled fruit and custard for tea, what a treat.

In some circumstances, families swapped items of food, especially if extra were needed for an event such as a wedding, the cake often home made would contain, fruit, sugar, butter and eggs among other ingredients. People tended also to use one shop, and their loyalty was often rewarded with specials, which were kept under the counter, this could be a little extra on the ration or, even a small tin of salmon. There was, as there still is in times of shortages, a black market racket, only people with money could take advantage of this and so, many were excluded. One of the main differences between then and now, is that there was very little exploitation, the cut throat mentality didn't really exist and, when it did, involved like minded individuals, all out to make themselves a bob or two.

Up until the fifties, whatever we could get hold of made a meal, food that would turn the stomachs of today's kids. Saturday night was the night for boiled pig's trotters, we would pick at the meat, it tasted like ham on the bone, which is exactly what it was. Fish and chip shops also sold cowheel, just that, cow heel!! They also sold tripe, which is cow's stomach, covered in salt and vinegar and eaten with hot chips – lip smacking. Sometimes it would be boiled with onions and served with a white sauce. Chickling was also available; these were actually cow's intestine. They literally had to be cleaned out and boiled. They never passed my lips, a bit too near to the rear end for my liking.

If you were either lucky enough or quick enough, a sheep's head could be had at the butchers. The brains would be removed and soaked in salt water. The membranous cover would be peeled away and the brains boiled.

A Proper Party.

They were grey in colour and had a very soft consistency. Once cooked, a knob of butter and seasoning added, they were mashed and served on toast. Other times we might have a pig's heart, which would be stuffed, roasted and sliced when cooled; this would make a good cold meat for sandwiches. Occasionally Dad would come home with wood pigeon. We had the job of plucking the feathers and removing whatever shot we could find. After cleaning out the izzards it was stuffed and roasted. They were eaten as poultry, though the meat was much darker than chicken, the taste was very similar. One of the more common dishes was rabbit hotpot. A fabulous pink flesh and so tender. Rabbits were freely available, young men would go out at night shooting rabbits and certainly not for the fun of it. They kept what they needed and sold the rest for a few pence. Mixamatosis in the seventies put paid to the rabbits. Fortunately, by that time, people were more prosperous and other food was freely available.

During the war, we were introduced to a tinned meat called SPAM, the name I believe is not an acronym. It looked and tasted something like luncheon meat. We either had it cold on sandwiches or, dipped in flour and fried, then eaten as a meat with vegetables. Sandwich filling, usually consisted of Shiphams or Princes meat and fish pastes. Other fillings were brown sauce, salad cream and for a sweet sandwich, condensed milk. The men always carried sandwiches for their lunches.

During and after the war, the Americans were never short of food, or so we were led to believe. We always had the impression, that it was the land of milk and honey. On occasions, they sent food over to their poor relations in the U.K. On one occasion, this was in the form of chocolate powder and a consignment was delivered to most schools. We were instructed to take a jam jar to school. Need I say that there were some really big jam jars and a good thing too? On our way home, we had a wonderful time, dipping our finger in the powder and sucking it. We were ages getting home, by which time the jar was half empty or, half full, whichever way you looked at it. Since our mother had no idea of the amount we'd been given, we got away with it.

Sunday was the only day we had breakfast, that is to say a cooked breakfast, rather than a piece of toast. Bacon was on offer, but you had to be quick, if you happened to be at the back of the queue, you got the dip. That was quite tasty, real dip, not like the watery stuff today. Oatcakes replaced bread on Sunday mornings. Oatcakes are special to Staffordshire, made using a secret recipe. It was savoury, not sweet, as its name might suggest. These would be collected freshly made; we always got ours

A Proper Party.

from Mrs Marrow, around the next street. The front room of her house, as in many terraced houses, was a sort of oatcake factory. A huge hotplate almost filled the room, and the mixture was kept in huge containers and ladled onto the hot plate. It was a very good business and there would be one on almost every other street.

Other than the Sunday oatcake, it would be bread. Always locally made and very crusty. If ever I was sent to get a loaf, I would pick off the crust as I made my way back home, the tastiest part I thought, and my reward for doing the errand. Sliced bread wasn't available and everyone was a dab hand at cutting the bread in straight slices, either thin, medium or thick according to what the bread would be used for. Sliced bread, when it came was a great time saver and everyone thought it was wonderful, hence the saying, " better than sliced bread". The art of bread slicing by hand was soon lost, cut fingers and thumbs reduced as a result.

In the late fifties and sixties, when food became freely available and more affordable, celebrations started to become commonplace, as in birthday and anniversary parties. That was when the tin of salmon came out as a must, along with the tin of peaches and carnation milk. Cold meat would generally be, sliced boiled ham, sliced ox tongue and jellied veal.

Around the turn of the seventies and eighties, the first foreign sounding food arrived, possibly French, it was Quiche Lorraine. One would hear gossip about a recent party, which went something to the effect of, "oh they had quiche Lorraine, it was a proper party", making the point, that if quiche Lorraine wasn't available, it wasn't a proper party. At that time, never in a million years, would we have thought about all the foreign foods we have now, and that smoked salmon and caviar would be common place

Until the sixties, small shops, which were actually a part of the family home were common place and were found on every street and corner. Generally they sold everything imaginable from, safety pins, gas mantels or electric light bulbs, bundles of sticks for the fire and groceries etc. These shops were part of our community and were used on a daily basis, for something or other. We knew the owners and they knew everyone they served on a personal basis. The shops were prolific and all very similar. They were quite small, often the front rooms of houses. Goods were stored on every available surface including the floor. The counter would be polished wood, well worn and all of a yard long, so, only one customer at a time could be served. There was

A Proper Party.

often no room for more than a couple of customers, which often meant a queue outside. Milk would usually be delivered to the door, either from the farmer, who carried the milk in churns on a cart pulled by a horse, or later, delivered in glass bottles by the local dairy. Other small shops would be more specialised, as in butchers, fish and chips or greengrocery etc.

On the high street would be well known names such as, Maypole, Home and Colonial, Redman's and the Co-op, they were all food shops. These tended to be slightly more upmarket than the corner shops. They tended to be larger and the food nicely displayed. Part of the counter housed the bacon slicer, cheese cutter and butter boards which were used to pat the requested weight of butter into a nice rectangular shape, before wrapping. Sides of bacon and ham would hang above the counter. Cold meat, cheese and butter would be kept under glass. Tea was also sold loose, weighed and packed in brown paper which was then tied up with a piece of string. Food was not pre packed, so we weren't paying for fancy packages. Loose goods such as fruit, would be put in brown paper bags.

In the late sixties the first so called super market arrived. The one that I remember was in Campbell Place, Stoke, and was called either Victor Value or Fine Fare. The floor space seemed huge in comparison to the shops that we had been used to. It was the first store where we used a basket and helped ourselves. Even so, by today's supermarkets, it was tiny, but, it heralded the death knell within a couple of decades, for the corner shops that we had come to know and love. What next, I wonder. Will these huge conglomerates survive the ever increasing technology, with its internet shopping, not forgetting the increasingly popular E-Bay.

THIS LITTLE PIG.

The children of the twenty first century are denied the freedom to roam, to enjoy nature in all its glory, throughout the changing seasons. A freedom taken for granted by the kids of the mid twentieth century, which I fear will never return.

The dangers of today were far from our minds, as we walked along the canal side, the cut as we called it. Past sideway, where often, youths would be swimming, that part of the cut was very warm, due to some outflow from the pit. We would be on our way to Trentham Park. Entrance was free; it was green open space, with large mature trees and a small, clear cold stream.

During our long summer holidays which always seemed to be dry and hot, was it rose tinted glasses or could we have had global warming more than half a century ago? It was wonderful to have the shade of the trees after an exhausting game of tick, which meant running after each other, over a wide area, or, to cool down with a paddle in the stream and catch the tiddlers which could be clearly seen swimming along. The more adventurous would be climbing the huge trees such as oak and horse chestnut, the latter providing the conkers in the autumn.

Play, wherever it was, would be interrupted for our fantastic picnic lunch, which consisted usually of bread and jam sandwiches, wrapped in greaseproof paper, there was no such thing as poly bags or cling film and tin foil. Liquid refreshment was in the shape of bottles of water. Corporation pop or Adams ale to us, usually the former, coming from a very religious family, ale was an unmentionable word, only used by drunken old men. The water would be passed around and everyone drank from the bottle, after a while, it was full of crumbs, a bit like the scenic snowflake souvenirs.

After a long day's play we would venture home, no doubt dawdling along, time unimportant. Our parents never worried too much about our return, it was a case of when we got home, we got home. Children were much safer in those days, abductions and murders were hardly heard of, there was abuse for sure but it was either accepted or brushed under the carpet.

Many days we would be sunburned, basic sundresses with a bib at the front and straps over the shoulders that crossed at the back were the order of the day, usually home made by mother. There was no such thing as covering up and certainly no sunblock. The only thing we had was calamine lotion to cool the skin down before we went to bed.

This Little Pig.

Fenton Park was on our doorstep. A legacy from the Victorian era, when the powers that be, decreed, that the poor peasants, slaving in hot, dusty and dirty factories should have an open space, which would be free to enter and would be maintained by the local authorities in perpetuity. For that reason, even today, most towns have the most beautiful formal parks. A refreshing space amidst urban sprawl. Our park was a sedate venue; no running around otherwise the park keepers had a stern word, more a stroll, admiring the diverse flora. Anyone who misbehaved would be shown the gate.

There was a grassy field towards the right, beyond the sunken rose garden. One year, gypsies set up camp there. I was really intrigued. Their horse drawn wooden vans were well cared for and highly decorated. They contained a polished iron stove which, I guess had a dual purpose of cooking and heating. Upholstered seats were lengthways on either side which would obviously convert to a bed. Hand made lace covered the small windows. The stable type doors were highly decorated inside and out. There were no toilets or baths, the kids were dirty and snotty nosed, not much different to many others. We wondered what they used for toilets and believe me, between a group of us our imagination ran wild. Being ill informed of others lifestyles, fosters much misunderstanding even today.

This Little Pig.

The horses were tethered and left to graze. The evenings saw them sitting around a fire, eating, drinking, laughing, singing and dancing. They seemed very happy with their lot in life.

The recreation ground or the rec was only minutes from home and we often ran over there. Played on the swings, roundabout, witches hat and slide of which there were two, a big one and a smaller one for the toddlers. We rolled down the embankment towards the railway line which was fortunately fenced. On our way to and from school we would walk through the rec as a short cut. It was a big wide open area, prone to the weather, either, very hot; very cold, very wet and the wind had a free reign. Hailstones would bite into the flesh, a stinging sensation on any exposed areas mostly the legs and face. Dried and chapped skin would be with us until spring. Unlike the park, this area has now been covered in residential properties.

The lido or Smiths Pool to give it its proper name was within a mile and easily accessible, an enormous area of undulating banks and ditches. To the left on entering the gate a bank rolled down to a small stream. In summer we would spend hours rolling down the bank, never to my knowledge ending up in the stream. In the winter, that area was the favourite place for sledging. Hoards of kids would congregate there, holding on to anything that could be used for sliding down the bank, a makeshift sledge in other words. This could be anything from a piece of plywood to a piece of corrugated tin with a piece of rope attached to the front, supposedly as an aid to steering, but gravity seemed to be the most important factor. There would be at least two or three kids, sometimes more to a so called sledge, most were off before it reached the bottom. There never seemed to be any injuries, it was up, brush off the snow and start again. The outdoor life, being exposed to all the elements toughened us up.

One summer in this very area, with a group of younger kids who, I was no doubt responsible for, we experienced an unusual occurrence. We busily played games, such as tick and ring a ring of roses, when a man was noticed sitting on the grass beside the railings. He seemed to be preoccupied with something and a few of the kids wondered off inquisitively. I somehow suspected what was happening and called them back, one of the kids said "he's got a little pig", yes, I thought, that's about right. He didn't really mean any harm and sauntered off, when he realised that nobody was interested.

The pool itself was quite big and it was possible to walk all the way around it. We were never short on exercise. Kids would fish and paddle, we never knew how deep it was because we never ventured too far, we were always told that there was a whirlpool in the middle, nobody was brave enough to test the theory. In winter it would freeze over and that meant time for skating. We were warned over and over not to go onto the ice, but, when did children ever take any notice of adults? The pool frozen over would be covered with kids who knew better than their elders. There were to my knowledge, a couple of tragedies and kids were eventually pulled from under the ice, drowned.

To the right towards Mount Pleasant was a larger area with a series of ditches. There we would jump from one side to the other, avoiding a drop in the middle. They were popular for hide and seek, just as long as you didn't disturb the couples enjoying a bit of hanky panky. In fact, these places were an education to us, especially as far as the birds and the bees were concerned, it was a subject never mentioned at home.

Almost every town had a public baths, not only a swimming pool but also baths which people used for a weekly or whatever, bath, when these facilities were not available in many homes. We would parade down to Stoke, sometimes with a fully blown inner tube from a lorry, cadged from Beckett's garage. We'd all muck about on and off the thing in the pool. We would only be allowed, when the pool was not being used by anyone else, which was quite often, we must have pitched it at the right time, we also knew the attendants and they kept a lookout for us. We had great fun and it didn't cost a fortune. The inner tube was the equivalent to a lilo or a fancy little ring, it lasted much longer too.

An uncle had an inflatable dinghy, we would carry this, already inflated down to the cut, all get in and paddle along. There was no fear of it being torn or damaged by underwater debris, it was always quite clean. There was no such thing as shopping trolleys and everything else found other uses, once their original purpose had been fulfilled. Anything that was in the cut was usually hauled up, generally by the police, dredging for a body, which wasn't that uncommon.

Usually, on summer Saturday afternoons, after our chores were done, we would go on a ramble with a group of young people, generally from the church. We had great fun as we walked to such places as Hilderstone, Lightwood and Rough Close. These destinations were chosen because they were within easy walking distance.

Occasionally a cycle ride was the order of the day. I had my first cycle when I was about ten. It was possibly my only cycle, since it was much too big for me. I can only assume, that it was brought with the intention that I would grow into it! My father taught me to ride, by taking me down to Carters Crossing. A straight road with hardly any traffic, it was crossed at the bottom as the name implies by a level crossing over the railway line. The cycle was held, while I mounted and sat on the seat. I was then given a good push and if I didn't remain upright, I suffered the consequences and there was no sympathy. I returned home with a huge bruise in the middle of my back from the end of the seat. It didn't take me long to ride properly. You never forget how to ride a bike, no wonder, the consequences would be more than another bruise or two.

Being able to cycle enabled our group to venture further afield, to places like Lichfield or Dovedale in the Peak district, an area of outstanding natural beauty. A valley, through which ran the fast flowing river Dove, bounded on all sides by hills. Caves were known to be in this area and a general search would reveal one or two. We entered with a mixture of trepidation and bravado, the latter turning to fear, as we frightened each other out of our wits. Stepping stones and a bridge, allowed the visitor, access over the river to the path on the other side. We dismounted and left our cycles in an area where the river widened near to the stepping stones, then it would be hill walking,

This Little Pig.

Thorpe Cloud being the highest. Or sometimes, just meandering along the riverside to the Manifold valley.

We always carried food and liquid refreshment, since it wasn't available in these places and if it had been, I doubt we could have afforded to buy it. Carrying food wasn't a problem, but, liquid wasn't always easy. In the absence of card or plastic containers, it was either a glass bottle or a thermos flask. Safely stowed, with the rest of my meagre gear in my saddle bag, I anxiously awaited my warm drink and was mortified, when I picked up my flask and it rattled, the glass lining had shattered. It must have been a bumpy ride.

PAPER BAUBLES.

Developing a taste wasn't an option, there wasn't time, this period of seemingly plenty didn't last long enough but never failed to appear and for certain foods we would have waited a whole year. It is what made Christmas so special. People saved what little they could throughout the year in order to have a good Christmas. It was a time to celebrate, not only the birth of Christ but in many cases either with a return of a loved one from the front line or surviving from the meagre rations allocated throughout the year.

Great effort went into the preparation and the decorations would start to go up early in December. The excitement was palpable and count down began. An old suitcase or a brown card board box would be brought out and the streamers along with the baubles and tree would be taken out. The streamers were huge, about six inches in diameter and were either square or round. They decorated the ceiling from centre to corner and centre to centre. The table usually situated in the centre of the room anyway, would be used to stand on in order to attach one end of the streamer using four drawing pins to the centre of the ceiling. A chair was then brought into play and would be dragged around the room according to where the other end was to be placed using the same method. Once these paper monstrosities were up the paper baubles came out. These were also quite huge when opened up and were

Paper Baubles.

usually in the shape of stars, bells or globes. They were hung in the spaces between the streamers. The festive season had arrived, it was like fairy land and the very young ones were lifted up for a better view. Everybody had a Christmas tree; it was rarely real and quite primitive in comparison to the artificial varieties of today. It was usually decorated with small cone shaped bags of dolly mixtures, nets of chocolate coins and chocolate ornaments covered with a decorated gold or silver paper. They looked very like the small glass baubles hanging beside which, appeared from the box year after year. There was a familiarity about Christmas, a sense of security, of continuity unlike the fashion of today where everything changes with the décor, silver and blue, red and gold, it is all so disposable.

Toys weren't plentiful but every child had something. Men had usually served an apprenticeship in one of the many trades and this would be put to good use before the big day arrived. The fret saws appeared and were used to produce wooden forts, garages, farm yards, dolls cots and exquisite dolls houses. These items were all painted quite professionally and in great style. The dolls houses would even have wall paper in some of the rooms. Furniture would be made from cardboard and covered in fabric which would also be used to hang at the windows for curtains. My father would melt lead and as a molten liquid it would be poured into moulds, when cooled, out would come fully formed lead soldiers. They were then beautifully painted usually in the colours of the military regiments. A lucky young boy would have his very own army albeit in pure lead, health concerns didn't figure in those days. Friends, relatives and neighbours, each with individual skills swapped and sold toys according to the wants and wishes of the others, nobody was out of pocket and nobody was disappointed.

The Christmas pudding and Christmas cake, only one of each was prepared well in advance. The pudding once mixed was wrapped in a muslin cloth and placed in a basin. It was then cooked by steaming for what seemed like hours on end. Once the cake was cooked it was covered in marzipan, using freshly ground almonds, specially imported for the season. It was then iced and decorated with small trees, robins, Santa Claus, snowmen, sledges and reindeer, all either made from plastic or plaster of Paris, a chalk like substance. Once the cake had been eaten and that didn't take very long, the decorations were washed and put in a drawer to be used and reused sometimes for generations. Small cakes such as mince pies and sponge fairy cakes were always made by Dad; he obviously inherited the talent from his father who worked in the family bakery. There

Paper Baubles.

would be little of the ingredients left in the bowl, but we would always manage to scrape a finger or two around it and suck of the gunge.
The goodies would be stored in a tin in the pantry and would be eaten over many days, almost rationed, we couldn't go and help ourselves, understandably, and I guess one can imagine the stampede.

For everyone, but especially the children, the build up to the big night and day was mind boggling. Santa wouldn't come if you were naughty and especially if you didn't go to sleep on Christmas eve, a very definite early night for the kids, much to the relief of the parents, who used the extra time to put the finishing touches to home made toys and to retrieve the toys that had been brought over a period of time and hidden in various locations around the house. Christmas Eve finally arrived as did the obligatory bath, one after the other; the kids would be in and out of the bath, youngest first. Then it was off to bed with the stocking, the bigger the better, this fact only seemed relevant to the older ones. With the stocking hung over the end of the bed, it was eyes closed and off to sleep because Santa was on his way, it would take a few years for reality to dawn on the little innocents. When morning finally arrived and like the kids today, we gingerly roused, not knowing whether or not he'd been and also knowing that if he hadn't, it was a double quick return to sleep. The older or braver would check the stocking for goodies and we would all be up. Every household in a similar situation, as lights started to appear in houses coming to life up and down the street. The contents of the stocking never varied, a few chocolate coins, a bag of sweets, an apple and an orange. Unbelievably, these items were real treats. The oranges were usually Maroque from Spain; they were wrapped in a fine blue or purple tissue paper, heaven for a few days as this replaced the squares of newspaper in the toilet; even our bottoms got a treat! Once downstairs we would all have a little pile of goodies, mainly consisting of one fairly substantial gift and other things such as an annual, colouring book and pencils, the latter being my favourite, I would spend all day, just colouring.

The turkey, cleaned, stuffed and placed in a large enamel cooking container would be taken early in the morning to Watson's bakery on Ashworth Street. Very few families had ovens large enough to hold a turkey and for this reason the local bakery opened its doors and ovens to the customers and cooked all the turkeys for free. They were collected a few hours later in time for lunch. During the cooking process and before we could partake, we had to attend the obligatory visit to church for the Christmas morning service. Most of the children, proudly carrying a new toy or book. The church service was usually followed by a visit to Grandma who always wallowed in our obvious excitement.

During this time, mother would return home to prepare the lunch and set the table. It would be a grand affair, the once a year job, complete with crackers containing paper hats which had to be worn and a small plastic toy or game. Nothing like the exotic Christmas crackers of today with their contents of trimmed hats and quality gifts. The cooked turkey, having been collected was carved in a traditional manner and would be served with home made sage and onion stuffing, sauces, roast and mashed potatoes, cauliflower, carrots and without fail, sprouts, they contained iron and were good for the blood, however, that didn't endear them to us, but plates had to be clean. If you couldn't eat your dinner, you couldn't eat your pudding and sure as hell we weren't missing out on that. All plates clean, the table tidied, the pudding was brought forth. No pyrotechnics were involved, either, the brandy was unaffordable or as in our house banned owing to the practice of prohibition enforced by mother. It was served with custard, not brandy butter or brandy sauce for the same reasons.

The afternoon would be relaxed as we were consumed in the new activities, in my case colouring pencils and book, my favourite pastime which would occupy me for hours.

Paper Baubles.

The highlight for the adults was the Kings/Queens Christmas message to all the citizens of the commonwealth which was broadcast on the radio until television became more widely available. Tea was taken late, since we were all so stuffed from a heavy lunch. The table remained set but was re-laid with a different variety of food. Cold turkey and stuffing sandwiches, slices of tinned Olde Oak Ham and the usual tinned salmon. The onions, pickled during the year would appear and we always had a trifle, devoid of sherry. The small home made cakes were placed on a three tiered cake stand and the precious Christmas cake had centre position until someone wanted a slice, it was then cut and that was that, it didn't last very long in our family, there were too many mouths.

The Christmas school break was welcome, it gave us time to enjoy our new gifts and also have a chance to enjoy a lie in and keep warm, to recharge our batteries in the middle of often very bad winters and since the Christmas fare lasted for a few days we were able to enjoy the extra treats. No such luck for the workers, there was no break between Christmas and New Year. After Boxing Day it was back to work, like it or not. New Years Eve was semi special, we went to the watch night service at church, somehow scared that the New Year might not arrive. It was a sombre occasion and we wondered if judgement day was only a few

Paper Baubles.

hours away. New Years day was not a public holiday, so again it was back to work, the kids had a few more days grace.

The streamers, tree and other decorations remained for the twelve days of Christmas; it was considered unlucky even for the religious to take them down before. When the time came and they were removed, the room opened up and became much brighter and lighter. There were so many pin holes in the ceiling from the drawing pins that it always had to be decorated after Christmas. The tree was taken down, very little was left to remove, since many of the decorations were edible and had disappeared over the previous days, the glass baubles were carefully packed away. The paper baubles and streamers including the dust were meticulously folded and along with all the other festive articles were put away for another day, another time, another year.

SNAKE'S OR EELS.

Few kids saw the sea until the late 50's. For this reason Stoke-on-Trent city council owned several properties in North Wales. They were convalescent or holiday homes and catered in their own way for various groups of people in the city. One such place was Rhyl homes, situated in Chester Street, Rhyl. It was meant for disadvantaged children, who needed a pick me up and a bit of colour in their cheeks. Our father worked for the council and often had to go to these homes to build extensions or to do repairs. Somehow, he managed to get us kids a week or two in Rhyl homes every year. It had to be sanctioned by a doctor, appointed by the council or education department and I guess being a big family was a good enough reason.

When the date for our holiday arrived, we had to wait by Fenton town hall, our cases packed and at the ready. The bus would arrive, we would duly board, our papers having been checked and we would be on our way. The first timers full of apprehension, some with a few tears as they bade farewell to anxious mothers, the old timers, full of excitement.

On arrival, we were checked for head lice and shown to our dormitory. There were the pink, blue, yellow and green rooms for the girl's, the boy's had the annex and the wooden hut. We were cared for by a team of so called nurses, some were qualified, especially Mrs Booth who was the matron at that time. All the staff had accommodation on the premises.It was quite regimented, but we had good plain healthy food based on three meals a day, eaten in a communal dining room, Formica topped tables, seating approximately eight kids to a table.

One day a week, we had a special outing to the fabulous Ffrith Beach in Prestatyn. Otherwise, we would have a daily walk to the beach. We would walk in a column of two's, maintaining a straight line. Regular holiday makers would eye us up and down. I guess they thought we were kids from a children's home, which, in a way we were, if only for two weeks.

As a family, we were very lucky, owing to our affiliation with the church, which incidentally, started life as Becketts mission. A place of worship, opened by a rather wealthy family who owned a garage and haulage business. One of the son's, owned a very nice bungalow in Kimnel Bay near to Rhyl, a popular destination, within easy reach of people from the potteries. For a very small sum we were allowed a two week stay there every summer. It was heaven, we would walk all the way along the beach to Rhyl, the soft sand enveloping our feet, as we ran back and forth shoeless. Rhyl, was such a beautiful, clean resort, as were all the resorts of North Wales in that era. It was self catering, much like home from home but with the benefit of plenty of fresh sea air and open space.

Another of the son's, had a very large eight berth caravan in Morecambe, Lanc's. It was situated on a very nice, well maintained site, just a short distance from the promenade. There were no disco's, bars or amusements that you find on the sites today. We would daily walk to the beach, whatever the weather and occasionally had a donkey ride.

A favourite activity was fishing from the jetty and we all had a go. On most day's we caught our tea which was plaice. They would be carried back to the caravan where they would be gutted, cleaned and cooked on the bone. Straight from the sea, the taste was out of this world, plaice never tasted the same since.

A regular catch was eels, my father would be hauling them in struggling for freedom. He would unhook them and they would wriggle all over the place. It was our job to grab hold of them and bang them over the head by any means to stun or kill them. They would be put in a container of sea water to be dealt with later! Due to his passion for oysters, and there must be something in the reputation they have, because he did father seven children! My father was very friendly with a fishmonger, who had an open fronted shop on the promenade. He did a deal with this guy, he would supply us with the small dishes of cockles and muscles, no doubt my father got the oysters and we would supply him, with freshly caught eels, on a daily basis for the duration of our stay. At the end of our fishing for the day, probably, coinciding with the receeding tide, the eels would be threaded by the mouth onto large safety pins. My brother and I, had the job of walking along the promenade to deliver the eels, they would be hung over our shoulders. We had lots of stares and comments from passers by, but, one stands out above all others. A young couple strolling along, hand in hand, caught site of us. The woman gasped, her eyes popped so far out of her head, she nearly lost them and exclaimed to all within earshot "look at those kids carrying snakes". My brother and I had a good laugh, and, in an instant grew a couple of inches in height, because we knew better than she did.

When we weren't fishing we would go rock pooling and shell collecting. The sand was fascinating, a bucket and spade was obligatory and we made good use of them. We would dig really deep holes and my father would say that we would be in Australia if we went any deeper. We made the most fantastic sand castles, ships and cars which the younger kids would sit and play in. A favourite game was burying each other in sand right up to our necks, we were all involved, from the youngest to the oldest. The only part visible, was a row of very happy faces, peering over the mounds of sand, all good inexpensive fun.

After a few years, the caravan owners sold up and moved to a really lovely bungalow in Heysham, just about a mile up the road from Morecambe. It was a pretty, interesting village. We did lots of exploring around Heysham and were fascinated by what we believed, were old Roman, marble coffins, in the graveyard a top of the hill, overlooking Morecambe bay. We still regularly walked to Morecambe jetty to do our fishing but, probably not as often, because it was only possible to fish when the tide was in, and, we found other things to do in and around Heysham.

There was quite a big dock side for one thing and vessels would traverse the Irish Sea to Belfast, Dublin and Douglas in the Isle of Man. There was always a midnight boat and several of my siblings were anxious for an adventure. That came one night in the form of walking to Heysham docks. Prior parental permission being sought and granted, we were comfortable in the knowledge, that we were not doing anything wrong. On arrival at the dock, we watched from a safe distance, the ship being loaded. Eventually it was the turn of the passengers to board. Singles, couples and families, many struggling with suitcases and packages. We assumed they must all be very rich people, to be going on what to us looked like an enormous passenger liner.

Once the ship set sail, we started our walk back, it was actually a fair distance to the docks. Once through the village, we came to the quite simple promenade in that area and were amazed, that we could see this magnificent ship, all lit up, gliding across the ocean, transporting all those people to some distant land. It was such a beautiful night, it was mid summer, the air was still and barmy. The tide was in and lapping the rocks below. We decided to sit on a bench and enjoy the moment. As we turned to go, I was aware of a lady at the rear of a house a top of the cliff. She did not beckon or speak to us. However, as we approached to cross the main road which ran parallel to the promenade, two police cars came screeching around the corner, and stopped beside us. They had been alerted by the lady, who thought, that a woman with a number of children appeared homeless. I explained what we had done and that we were on our way back to our accommodation, where our parents were awaiting our return. They were quite happy that we were O.K. and capable of making our own way, the short distance back. They bade us goodnight and left. Our adventure was recounted many times during the following days. Heysham became our holiday destination for many years and many fond memories remain of the time spent there.

The minister at our church, had family in Finaghy, Belfast, Northern Ireland. In our late teens, a friend and I would visit these lovely people. The journey necessitated crossing the Irish sea and we did so, from the docks in Heysham. Memories of that adventure years before, came flooding back as I, became one of those rich people, boarding the liner, which looked much smaller than it did that time long ago.

We had a wonderful time, always quite restful, with lots of invites from other people in Belfast. They were all so very friendly and hospitable. We got to travel around and see such beautiful places as the fairy glens of Antrim, it was a little hilly, lots of ferns and moss. A huge canopy of hardwood trees gave shade, the sound of rippling streams and waterfalls and the earthy dank smell, stays in my nostrils to this day. The seaside resort of Carrick Fergus, genteel,quaint and clean, Donegal and Lisbon, all so welcoming. Often we visited the river Lagon, where, for the first time I heard talk of IRA activity. We would walk the Malone Road, past enormous houses, obviously the homes of the monied people. Our friends accommodation was a first and second floor maisonette on a council estate. It could not have been more homely or comfortable, had it been a stately home.

We attended the fisherman's mission on a Saturday night and enjoyed the walk around Belfast, browsing in the many junk and antique shops. This was quite a time before the troubles, which, once started would continue for decades. It pained me to see on TV these lovely friendly people, so bitterly divided. The Shankhill and other thorough-fares, that I had walked so freely, became no go areas. The friends we stayed with, sadly passed away and I lost touch with people we met, but, they were often in my thoughts and I wondered how they had fared during that awful period.

During the forties and fifties, Butlins and Pontins holiday camps were very popular. They catered for the working classes and enabled many, an annual holiday for a very moderate charge. Everything was included, accommodation, food and plenty of entertainment. Billy Butlins idea was, that everyone could have a holiday, for the equivalent of an average week's wage.

In the sixties, people started to become a bit better off, jobs were plentiful and Spain, started to become a popular destination. You were really doing well, if you were one of the masses going to the Costa Brava. A resort abroad for the working classes, a step up from Butlins or Pontins. The accessibility of the Costa Brava, was made possible by a firm called Airtours. A company which started small, it was rumoured, they had one aircraft, which flew backwards and forwards to Spain. It had a reputation for breaking down and at times, was the butt of many a joke. From small acorns grow mighty oaks and they must have known what they were doing, from that small beginning, a multi million pound business, now takes millions of tourists, many working class, all over the world.

THE THICK AND THE THIN.

School started at age four and half, usually in the nursery. It wasn't necessary to put the children's name down on a waiting or admission list. It was assumed, that the children would attend the nearest school in their area and, as a general rule this is what happened. Either, places were available or found. Parents just turned up at the school, when the child reached the appropriate age, registered and handed the child over, simple, what's gone wrong ?.

Our local school was Manor Street and we started off at little manor. The nursery, being the introduction to our educational life. It was a well equipped little place and in the afternoon, folding beds, which were constructed of wooden poles and canvas, would appear along with a small blanket. The kids recognised their own bed, by the symbols on the beds and the blankets. These, could be anything from a kite to a boat. Every child was allocated a symbol on admission, this was carried through to coat hangers and play aprons etc. All the kids had a little rest, whether they slept is another matter, I guess they all did at some point or other. Talking was not allowed, the silence no doubt golden.

Following the nursery, we then progressed through the infants, class by class, according to age not ability, though I guess we were all pretty average, infact, quite smart, our short

69

life had taught us that much. As we learned to write, we were given our own piece of slate. It was surrounded by a wooden frame. On one occasion, we were asked to take them home for a bit of maintenance. My father, French polished mine and when I returned to school on Monday morning, I handed it over, quite proud that my father had done such a good job. My teacher at the time, asked if my father would be prepared to French polish them all? I'm pleased to say, he did. It was a happy school; our head was Miss Bullock and among our teachers were Miss Roberts and Mrs Millenchip. We always walked to and from school, unaccompanied by parents and often through the rec', a short cut. Walking was compulsory, hail, rain or shine. It kept us fit and used up all those calories from the beef dripping; we'd had on toast for breakfast. Little manor, so called because it was alongside big manor, the local girls secondary school. It was not uncommon, for siblings to be at both schools at the same time. We attended the infant's school, until the age of seven, when we moved to the junior school.

Church Street, Church of England School, was the junior school in our area. This was much different from our lovely infant's school. We had more to learn, had to be more responsible and we had the cane. Our head was Mr Gumbley, a kindly, elderly man, even though

The Thick and The Thin.

he gave me the cane most mornings. Anyone late for registration was sent to stand outside his office and I was a regular. He would appear, with his short thick cane and we were given one stroke, across the palm of either right or left hand. Excuses were never proffered; it was a foregone conclusion, that they were not required. I always felt aggrieved by this punishment.

It was my job, as the oldest of seven children, to take the younger ones as they came of school age and deliver them, to their appropriate classes each morning. As their school opened at the same time as mine, obviously, I couldn't be in two places at the same time. I always saw them inside, with their coats hung on the correct peg. I would then run for my life, from Manor Street along Church Street, crossing a busy main road between the two, to my own class. Always late, and at times, bleeding from a fall, a couple of scars remain as a reminder, not of the run, but of the cane and the injustice.

It was recognised as a very good school. The teachers were excellent and I suppose for the time quite fair, though I expect, that would be questioned in today's society. Among our teachers were, Miss Jones, Mrs Colclough, Mr Earnest and Mrs Mackinnon. Mr Frost and Mr Mellor along with Miss Moore occupied another building, which housed the heads office and staff room.

Miss Moore was old, especially to me. She had also taught my mother before me, so I guess she was knocking on a bit. She was very tall and thin and always wore black pointed lace up shoes. She was almost witch like, she lacked the broomstick, but had a very lethal cane. We were eleven year olds by the time we reached her class, feeling our feet a bit I suppose. Any dissent would quickly be knocked on the head, by way of the wooden blackboard rubber, flying over the classroom. If you were quick enough, you ducked and it hit the person sitting behind. She also had another weapon in her armoury. It came in the form of a very long thin cane. She would whoosh it through the air a few times, before actually hitting your palm, it made a loud whistling sound, as she brought it down with speed. This treatment would be metered out, for such misdemeanours as talking or chewing gum. Some teachers certainly had a sadistic streak. Discipline was important and necessary, but was brute force? Some of the lads were known to get several strokes of the cane on bare backsides.

We had to write, using pen and ink. Monitors would bring ink wells around in the mornings and place them in the holes provided in the desks. They would be collected at the end of the day and refilled. The monitors were regularly ribbed by the other kids, as teacher's pets or goody goodies. The ink had more than one use. If we thought, that a particular teacher had been a bit over the top, one of the kids on the front row, would flick ink on the teacher, while their back was turned towards the class when writing on the blackboard. So, we did at times get our own back. Generally, we all stuck together, and nobody but nobody, would own up to committing the crime or even, to being a witness to such a thing, in which case, we all got punished.

In our time, all school children were provided with school milk. It was actually a third of a pint and was handed out each morning. It came in individual glass bottles which had a cardboard top, a small hole could be punched out, in the middle, through which a straw would be put. We would collect these tops. A common sight in the playground was a group of girls, sitting against the wall, on the concrete playground, a ball of wool and a few tops in hand. We would make the most beautiful pom poms. These would often be seen, hanging from the hoods of prams and cots. They would make safe toys and provide some amusement, for babies and young children. If we weren't doing that, we would be improving our skills at cat's cradle, skipping, netball, tick or hopscotch.

The Thick and The Thin.

The boy's and girl's playgrounds were separate. It seemed so important to keep us apart, in some ways this made us more curious, which, is when we found out that the boy's playground housed the rather large air raid shelters. There was often a bit of rudimentary medical practice in there after school, a game conveniently called, playing doctors and nurses.

School nurses made regular, unannounced visits to schools. Mostly, to check our hair. Anyone found to have head lice, was immediately excluded and was only readmitted when clean. Ring worm was common, anyone found to have that, had to have their head shaved and a purple coloured lotion called gentian violet was applied. It was a real shame for these kids; they were ridiculed something rotten and avoided like the plague. It was nothing more than a fungal infection, probably spread by over crowding and poor housing. It would be treated far differently today, probably with oral medication. During my time at little manor, I spilled tea down my front one morning and it stained my vest. I was unlucky enough, to get a visit from the school nurse that very day and was admonished, for having a dirty vest. I was petrified for ages after and if I ever saw the nurse I made a run for home.

About twice a year, the school medical officer came to school. Our parents would be

The Thick and The Thin.

informed of the impending visit and asked to attend, to accompany their child for this routine medical examination. Our height and weight were checked. Heart and lungs sounded, throat checked, along with any absences from school and the medical reasons. If any abnormality was found during these examinations, a suitable referral was made, to either, local doctor, hospital or optician.

An annual visit from the school dentist was certainly not met with glee. If any cavities were found, we were asked to attend for treatment at the school dental clinic in Stoke. A foreboding place, devoid of anything bar Spartan, tubular metal chairs. The walls were covered in brown tiles with a green tile border. The glass in the windows was frosted. No one could see in and by the same token, no one could see out. The only distraction was the terrified faces of the other kids, mirroring your own. Members of the medical and allied professions were never taught bedside manners, let alone how to communicate with children, we were non existent entities, talked about, not talked to. The old adage, children should be seen and not heard, springs to mind. Situations and procedures were never explained. Fear of the unknown was far worse than could ever be imagined. What teeth weren't extracted by the correct method at the dentist, were pulled out using a piece of string and a door knob at home. The other down side, was that there were no rewards, tooth fairies hadn't been created.

Church Street school, accommodated everyone that wasn't a roman catholic, they attended the local catholic school nearby. On reflection, bigotry has always, and unfortunately, will always exist. If we met at the end of the school day, there would be such cat calls as catholic bulldogs or churchy bulldogs. Catholicism to my mother, who was a strict Wesleyan type, was as good as the anti Christ. We weren't even allowed to walk down Havelock Street, the street on which the Catholic Church was situated and we stayed a mile away from the corpus Christie procession. Many cities have two main football clubs, this actually stems from the fact, that Protestants supported one and Catholics supported the other. Thank God that most people have seen some sense.

The late forties saw the first wave of immigration. An Indian lad called Autar Singh, Sikh by religion, was in my class at school. He had a hanky tied around a little top knot of hair. He was a likeable boy. His family lived near to me and their difference fascinated me. I was interested in their clothes and what they ate and also how they lived. Most of these people, earned their living selling a variety of goods from leather suitcases, door to door. The fore runner, of the door to door salesmen employed by the likes of Kleeneze and

The Thick and The Thin.

Betterware. They carried cases, which when opened, displayed a selection of waxes, polishes and cloths, hoping for a sale. A far cry from the glossy catalogues left at the door today.

At the end of the school day, we would run onto the potbanks. Most of the kids had a parent or other relative working there. The kids and however many of their friends, just stayed with their relative until knocking off time, a sort of child minding on the cheap. We were adept at flower making, painting and lithographing. My maternal step grandmother was a Mrs, the term used to describe a supervisor, of the sponging and fettling shop, at Grimwades, Stoke, also known as Carlton Ware. I often spent time in the school holidays there, and became a dab hand at sponging and fettling, mostly cup handles. We were never paid, because we were never officially employed. We did it because we loved it and, to some extent, it made us feel grown up. Pot banks were like rabbit warrens. Built on two or three floors, with numerous wooden staircases, inside and out, between the floors. Cobbled yards gave access to the bottle ovens, biscuit saggars piled up at the sides. The yards, criss crossed all day, by men carrying ware for firing, on six foot long planks, between the clay shops and the bottle oven. Our sojourns on the pot banks came to an abrupt end overnight, with the introduction of the factories act, which banned kids. They were obviously very dangerous places, but the practice had been going on for generations. It hit some families very hard, since they had to make alternative child care arrangements.

Our days at the junior school ended on reaching the age of eleven. The sexes were then completely segregated, the boys going to one school and the girls going to another. Even the ones that passed the eleven plus exam went separate ways, the girls going to the high school and the boys to the grammar school. For the rest in our town the boys went to Duke Street and the girls to Fenton Manor. At eleven, we were considered quite grown up and had to find our way around, what seemed to us a rather large school but no comparison to the comprehensives of today. Different subjects were taught in different classrooms and for the first time in our lives we had time tables. It took a couple of weeks for us to sort out where the next lesson was and corridors were like Crewe junction at the rush hour, as we hurried about, getting our bearings. Besides the main subjects such as reading, writing, maths, history and geography, it was important that we learned to sew and cook. The boys were taught metal work and woodwork. On the whole, a very rounded education, interesting and enjoyable. Not only were we allotted class places, we were also put into houses. There were four, so called houses

The Thick and The Thin.

in our school. All named after female saints, each signified by name and colour. Saint Bride, blue. Saint Ursula, yellow, Saint Hilda, red and Saint Cecelia, green. I was in the latter house, the patron saint of music. Every year, we made pictures of the Saints, they were hung in the school hall. We had huge wooden boards which would be covered, in a clay like substance. The appropriate saint, along with a suitable background was outlined in the clay.
We would gather as many different coloured petals, moss, bark and leaves as possible. These would be pressed into the clay, according to colour and texture, to create a sensational picture. This technique is used throughout north Staffordshire and Derbyshire to create the famous annual well dressings.

Once in school, I would always try to sit near to the window. In the summer the sun was welcome and comforting. Along that wall, ran the huge heating pipes, so it was one of the warmest places in the winter. The cold feet soon got warmed up on the pipes and before the teacher arrived, so did the bottom. If we were caught, we were sternly warned about the risk of piles and chilblains. I can say with some certainty, there is no truth in that old wives tale. It was common for a girl at this school to start her periods. Often the only information any of us had, regarding this act of nature, was from our class mates.Some of the descriptions of the impending, inevitable event were hair raising. Things of this nature weren't talked about, other than between friends. So, we suffered in silence until we got the show! Our head mistress was a Miss Wilkinson, Ophelia was her first name, and it takes little imagination to appreciate, what we made of that, oh feel here, springs to mind. She was stern and not very approachable, but when necessary could be exceptionally kind. If our period started while we were in school, we would have to attend her office. Following an explanation of our situation, she would present us with an enormous, sanitary towel and a piece of string. She was known to warm the towel, which made it more comforting, in front of the coal fire which was always aglow in her office.

It was at this time, that sex and the consequences of it became understood. Though it was never openly discussed, human nature hasn't changed since Adam was a lad. If a young man could get his leg over, he was lucky, they tried hard enough and would use all manner of reasons as to why it was OK. I was once in conversation with a neighbour of ours and the subject of swimming came up. I told him that I could swim a length, his reply was, that I was old enough to take a length. The answer was a very definite NO, the only contraceptive, against an unwanted pregnancy, which would bring shame on the girl and her family. In many cases, the hapless lass, would be dispatched to a home for unmarried mothers. There, she would give birth, with little or no sympathy and her baby would be taken for adoption. Though this was severe, it was an improvement on a few decades earlier, when she would have been placed, in a mental institution for life. Many of these poor women, only knowing freedom, when the mental health act changed and the wards were unlocked, inmates allowed out; a privilege, most found disconcerting, following years of being institutionalised. The same punishment didn't apply to the opposite gender.

At fifteen, school days ended for most, we were adults and had to earn a crust. Work beckoned and the family wanted a return on their fifteen year investment.

Above: Me as a baby with my mother and soldier father.

Left: With my swing in our back garden at High Street East, (City Road) Fenton.

Above: Our neighbourhood V.E. Day party. Me on the
front row in my home made Union Jack suit.
Below: On the stage at our Sunday School Anniversary,
the girl on the far left third row up is me.

Left: A group of neighbourhood children on the roundabout at the rec.

Right: A make believe May Queen and attendants parade down the backs.

Left: A note from our M.P. Ellis Smith, acknowledging a letter that I wrote to him expressing my concerns about the H. Bomb.

Right: A copy of my letter to the House of Commons along with a photograph appeared in the Daily Herald on 13th April 1954.

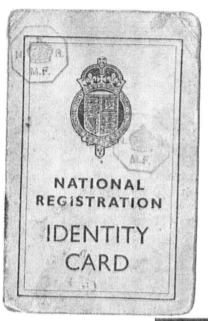

Left: My original identity card.

Right: The culmination of a successful state education. Myself as a very proud State Registered Nurse.

A BUTTON OR A PIN.

Toy's weren't in plentiful supply, certainly not the high tech' gadgets of today. A lack of toys didn't prohibit play, we just used our imagination. One of the biggest differences was that gender and stereotyping, played a much bigger role in the availability and distribution in the toy's that we had.

For the girls it was the obligatory doll, which was made of celluloid, a substance that easily dented, sometimes permanently, according to the force of the kick. If you fell out with a sibling, watch your doll, it might get used as a football. Some were crying babies, a mechanical device, fitted inside the doll which emitted a type of baby cry, as the doll was tilted backwards and forwards. The faces including the eyes were painted on. Only, when the rubberised dolls came along, did the sleeping eyes, these could get pushed to the back of the head, by a vexatious or jealous friend.

The clothes were usually knitted affairs, often the handiwork of grandma. They were a smaller version of baby clothes and any female worth her salt, was adept at knitting these. We used baby feeding bottles; they were really pretty and quite dainty. A sort of elongated 'U' shape, with an opening at either end, a rubber cap was fitted to one end and the feeding teat to the other; they were so easy to hold.

A Button Or A Pin.

We often had a dolls cot, of excellent quality, usually hand made by family members who were carpenters or joiners, craftsmen who had served a seven year apprenticeship, knew their trade well and took great pride in their work. Dolls prams were wonderful, perfect replica's of the real thing. The two major manufacturers being Pedigree and Silver Cross, the product almost identical, enamelled, coach built bodies on sprung chassis. They must have been a very comfortable ride and were a pleasure to push. Far superior to the prams of today, which I appreciate are made with the car in mind. That can't be faulted either, since shopping or housing is now out of town. A far cry from the terraced houses and corner shops.

Our playmates would be our neighbours and since we all attended the same school they were also our classmates. Of course, there were the odd fall out's and some of the parents had a set too. Often to no avail, since the kids would be friends again almost before the final vitriolic verbals had rolled off the tongue.

The service road, the backs as we called it, which ran between the backs of the rows of houses, was our playground. Groups of lads would be playing marbles or shotties, small glass balls with a colourful twist in the centre. The bigger ones were called ally's. I can only describe it as being a miniature bowls. One player trying to knock the other player's shottie off target. These games could and often did go on all day. One of my brothers actually wore a hole in his thumb nail, from constantly playing this game. He had enormous amounts of shotties, because the winner had the pick of the opponent's shotties including his ally's. My brother was one of the best, feared by his rivals but he did have plenty of practice.

Some of us would put three to four house bricks on top of each other; these would support the dustbin lid which would be leaned up against them. This acted as the wicket, as we played a game of cricket using a piece of wood and any old ball.

The more adventurous, climbed the six foot walls, that bounded the back gardens and would run the length of the backs, along the coping stones, jumping over the gaps that formed the gateways. The neighbours didn't complain, because everybody had kids and they were all involved.

Skipping was tremendously popular as a group sport; we often used an enormous washing line. A child at either end turning the rope and as many as ten kids in synchronized jumping. The more adept engaged in French skipping, which involved the use of two ropes being turned in opposite directions. We had regular races and a game of tick or tag, either down the backs, or on the road that ran along the bottom of the backs, Napier Street it was called but was, in fact an unmade road. The woman living in the bottom house, adjacent to Napier Street, couldn't tolerate the site of us kids and would always, come out and send us off. We weren't disturbing anyone, it was a large area and virtually free of traffic due to its condition. Her behaviour caused us to rename the road to Queen Martha's Highway.

Collecting cigarette cards was a hobby everyone enjoyed. Not only was it collecting but it also involved some canny wheeling and dealing. The cards displayed pictures and information on celebrities either sports people or film stars. Clarke Gable was one of my heart throbs. The cards were collected from packets of bubble gum or packets of sweet cigarettes, sticks of white toffee, possibly very hard icing, with a pink tip at one end. They would be eaten but not before we'd had a good long smoke, imitating the drawing in and blowing out of the smoke, definitely banned today. We spent hours sorting the cards, swapping the one's that we'd doubled up on for the one's that we lacked. It kept us in touch with our peers, a shared interest, and common camaraderie.

One or two stray dogs would occasionally be around. A copulating pair, a source of great entertainment for us but it wouldn't be long, before one of the neighbours, would be throwing a bucket of cold water over to separate them. Did it embarrass the adults?

A game of conkers would always be on the go. They would be harvested in the autumn, soaked in vinegar and cooked in the oven. The centre would then be drilled, a piece of string threaded through and they would be hung until required. The harder they were, the better, since the champion was the one who smashed the most conkers. I understand that this game is now banned from schools for health and safety reasons. This organisation has a lot to answer for. I can't ever remember, anyone getting injured from a conker. Kids were taught to protect themselves in those day's and rightly so. We didn't depend on the nanny state, which seems to have stripped everyone of common sense, leaving many kids, with an inability to make any decisions, which might carry an element of risk.

At the top of our road there was quite an incline, which followed the curve of the corner. We would come careering down there on anything that had wheels. During the winter, we'd spend hours, compacting snow and making a real ice slide. It was mostly the lad's that would run and then, sideways would slide on the ice, down the road, usually upright. We didn't think at the time, but now wonder what happened to the elderly? They must have avoided it, knowing that it was there as an annual occurrence. The only other people to traverse that area, would be the drunks as they turned out of the pub, which fronted the slide. I suppose if they fell, they either wouldn't feel it or would be unable to decide, whether the ice or the intoxication was to blame.

We would play out at night but under a nine o'clock curfew and always within a few yards from home. On the dark winter nights, we'd play knock and run. We'd knock on somebody's door and then run and hide. Sometimes we would tie two knockers together, knock on both doors and watch, as each one struggled to open the door, often cursing us little buggers. There was one corner shop, just at the top of our backs. It was run by an old lady and her son. Open boxes of sweets were displayed in the window, which were covered over with tissue paper, when the shop closed in the evening. We had a great time at night, tapping on the window, trying to attract the attention of the mice as they scampered over the paper. We were the vandals of our day, but, let the policeman show up and we were dead scared. We'd get taken home and a good thrashing was the order of the day or night. If our parents ever knew, that we had caused any annoyance or used our lip, being rude in other words, we had the strap across our backsides and were made to apologise.

Swings, slides and climbing frames were only seen in places like the rec, never in private gardens. My mother was a fanatical gardener and our garden was a show both back and front. No place for us kids to run around; a punishment would await anyone of us, who put a foot, on one of the borders. We never got bored and older kids were responsible for the younger ones. Bigger families ensured built in baby sitters for years. This involved every waking or playing hour. I spent so much time, particularly with the youngest two, of my six siblings that I was asked if they were my children, reasonable, I suppose, considering I was well in my teens when the youngest was born. I had an old head on my shoulders and hard skin on my hands.

Pocket money was hard to come by and had to be earned, the tooth fairy wasn't around. We could put our hand to anything, running errands, bringing, carrying and fetching for a penny or two. Then down to one of the many corner shops. A favourite was Atkinson's or Acko's. We preferred their sweets to the one's that came with extras, courtesy of the mice. Choice depended on how much we had. The cheapest were tiger nuts. A sort of dry, shrivelled pine nut, once mixed with a bit of spit, became quite sweet and juicy. Arrowroot,

A Button Or A Pin.

usually kept in jars was a fibrous stick with a very specific taste. It was chewed and sucked until it was totally dry and devoid of flavour. Otherwise, favourites were fairy satins. A small boiled sweet, triangular in shape, in the most beautiful, delicate, shimmering colours. The taste had a mild hint of fruit. Tom thumbs, very small, multi coloured, chewy gums. Cherry lips, red lip shaped gums with a cherry flavour. Gob stoppers lasted days and changed colour as the layers dissolved. We often had sticks of hard liquorice and a bag of kai-ly, otherwise known as sherbet or lemonade powder. The liquorice was dipped in the kai-ly then sucked. A substitute was a stick of rhubarb and a saucer of sugar, eaten the same way, had the same effect.

During the long summer holidays, a few kids would get together and arrange to put on a show. The morning would see us rehearsing our dancing, singing and reciting routine. The show would be held in someone's back yard. A makeshift stage would be erected, word would get around that a show was imminent. Admission was by producing a button or a pin; it wasn't unknown for kids to pull the buttons from their clothes to gain entry. The entertainers, dressed up in whatever they could find, maybe the odd fox fur or fancy hat and the show began. There always a huge crowd and it would be a good way, to keep many kids occupied for a couple of hours or

89

so. Whatever happened to all those buttons and pins, I wonder.

WHITER THAN WHITE.

The bang of the gas boiler being lit, signalled seven am, Monday morning, wash day. Monday was the universal washday in our neighbourhood. It could never be done on any other day. Perhaps something to do with Sunday best being returned to the pawn shop for another week. This happened in quite a few families, especially in the earlier decades of the twentieth century. Everything in the house that had to be washed was washed. As we got older we had to strip off our beds and deliver the sheets etc to the kitchen, which was set up for the day.

The centre table was pushed to one side, and in its place were two, barrel shape, free standing galvanised zinc tubs and dolly pegs, one tub for washing, manually filled with hot water, usually carried from the boiler using a bucket. Blocks of hard soap were grated into the hot water and dissolved. It was in the late forties and fifties before powdered soap came along, there wasn't much choice for many a year and the first one's on the market had names such as Acdo, Rinso, Oxidol and Tide. My favourite came later and was called Dreft, it was tiny squares of very fine soap and was used for delicate fabrics, it was so soft and had a feel of fine confetti. The other tub was filled with cold water and was used for rinsing, often a blue bag was added to the water, it produced a bluish tinge and made the whites look whiter than white. In between the tubs stood the mangle which consisted of two rubberised rollers atop a stand, the early rollers were huge wooden things. A large screw above the rollers applied or released the pressure as required. The rollers were attached to a couple of cogs, which were operated by turning a rather large handle.

The cast iron boiler took up a big corner of the bathroom, which was situated on the ground floor, next to the kitchen. The boiler was a permanent fixture with its own gas supply. It was covered by a heavy wooden lid. It had to be filled by hand and a large newspaper taper, lit from the gas cooker or stove as it was called then, was carried into the bathroom and the huge gas jet of the boiler was ignited.

All the whites were boiled and were the first to be washed. After boiling, the linen was lifted out of the boiler using large wooden tongs. It was then put into the tub containing the soapy water. Then the hard graft began, using the dolly peg, it was pounded, turned and twisted until it was considered clean. It was really labour intensive, and if women hadn't found themselves pregnant so often, no doubt they would have had beautiful hour glass figures. Heavily soiled clothes especially, the collar and cuffs of working shirts were scrubbed before washing, this was done using, a block of hard soap, a scrubbing brush and a scrubbing board, the early ones were wooden, the later ones were galvanised zinc. The metal boards were in great demand in the fifties and sixties when they became a musical instrument in the skiffle groups which were popular at that time. After washing, the linen was lifted, put through the mangle and into the rinsing tub where it was again subjected to another pummelling. It was folded as it was lifted out of the rinsing water and again put through the mangle, the folding made ironing a little easier. It was then ready to be put on show, most Monday's the washing was hung outside on the line which stretched the length of the garden or yard. Lines of washing hung the length of every garden, the length of the street. It was almost a competition, neighbours judged each other by quality, quantity and colour. There would be more than a nudge, nudge, wink, wink as they eyed the fluttering wares. Any stains or greyness and the elbows went in, "hers a dirty bugger her is", an epitaph nobody wanted.

Besides the tubs, there was a big bowl of starch, Robin brand was the usual, it came in a small white box which had blue writing and a robin on the front. It was made by dissolving the powder in cold water and then adding hot water until it was the required thickness. If this process was incorrectly performed it would all go lumpy. Many cotton items were starched; it gave them an extra crispness and repelled the dirt for a little while longer. On rainy days, the washing could be in and out several times. There were no driers, except the open fire. In the winter, wet laundry was hung over a wooden frame known as a clothes maid or clothes horse. This was positioned in front of and around the fire. The steam that this process gave off pervaded the whole house and everything felt damp. The warm damp smell of washday hit the nostrils. Even in winter outside drying might be attempted with heavier items. The result often caused some amusement, when the clothes were brought back inside, and they could stand up on their own, frozen solid.

Washday was dreaded especially in winter, we returned from school, cold to the bone, dying to get warm, by the only source of heat in the house. Hearts sank when we discovered that the fire was totally hidden by a bank of damp clothes. The clothes maids had a much better use as far as we kids were concerned. In the summer, when they weren't needed around the fire, they were upended in the garden, covered with a sheet or old blanket and hey presto, we had a tent.

The kitchen floor had red quarry tiles, which was just as well, because the water really slopped around and we almost had to paddle through it. At some point in the early fifties my mother became the proud owner of a jiffy. It was the fore runner of the washing machine. A square metal casing housed a drum which held hot soapy water and the items to be washed. The lid had an agitator on the under side and a handle, with a knob at the end, was on the top. The lid was placed on top of the drum with the agitator inside. The handle was moved in a forward and backward motion, this in turn moved the agitator. The jiffy also came with an inbuilt mangle, which was a much sleeker version than the ones on a stand.

Ironing was done on a Tuesday and flat irons were used. These were heated by rotation on a stand in front of the fire or on the stove. The temperature was measured by spitting on the iron, when the spit sizzled and evaporated, the irons were hot. They were held using a piece of padded fabric which prevented a burnt palm. They were very cumbersome and certainly not as sleek as the later electric models, but, clothes were beautifully pressed. Ironing was an art, passed down the generations; it demanded skill and plenty of elbow grease. A damp cloth was often used between the iron and certain fabrics to obtain a better crease, or, prevent scorching. Any clothes found to be in need of mending or buttons needed replacing were put aside, to be attended to later, usually in the evening. Ironing boards were quite primitive wooden contraptions, in most households, a blanket was folded and placed on the kitchen table, just as good as it provided a bigger working area.

The house was always cleaned on a Saturday morning. We had no fancy implements just the basics. Pegged rugs were thrown outside to be beaten; this got rid of a week's dirt and debris. We were taught to clean from top to bottom, front to back. If the bedrooms were on the agenda, that's where we started, but they weren't cleaned that often. If there were any guzunders or chamber pots they definitely had to be emptied, a week was long enough!!!. In some houses a zinc bucket replaced the chamber pots. I had a friend who I often stayed with, on a Saturday night as I got older, her father thought nothing of swinging the bucket, as he walked through the living room towards the stairs, on his way to bed. Whatever odours that were undoubtedly produced by these bodily fluids was dissipated in a fashion by the use of air fresheners. These came in round blocks of crystallised air freshener, a product that has survived to this day. Ours were kept in small round plastic doilies. It was a pastime of ours, sewing two of these doilies, by threading narrow ribbon through the openwork pattern, leaving a gap at the top and a loop of ribbon. The air freshener was put inside this fancy container and hung on a nail or hook as required. We enjoyed making these holders and would even make tiny plastic flower decorations or bows on the front. It was one way of making a few pennies, because we found a market, especially among older neighbours.

On a weekly basis, we started the cleaning on the landing, using a hand brush we swept the carpet and the white painted wood on either side of the runner. When we got to the bottom, all the dust was swept into a dustpan. The small hall had a quarry tiled floor; this was polished with red cardinal. It was a red polish which came in a tin. It was applied evenly with a cloth, when dry it was polished to a shine, it wasn't an easy job and seemed to take an age.

In the living room, top to bottom meant polishing the furniture. After removing the ornaments and vases of plastic flowers, Mansion polish was used to get rid of the dust, it was applied sparingly so that it was easier to polish to a shine. If too much was applied, it dried with a smoky grey type haze. In the bay window we had a drop leaf table; a dining room chair was placed on either side. On the back wall was a piano, Dad was quite a good pianist. Opposite the window was a big oak sideboard, which consisted of a cupboard on either side and drawers down the middle. The very best possessions were housed in this piece of furniture. On either side of the chimney breast stood a china display cabinet and a bookcase. Quite a lot of polishing and more than enough plastic flowers. In the

Whiter Than White.

centre of the room was a three piece suite, ours was a sort of grey rexine, a heavy oilcloth, plastic material, it had an engraved pattern and red piping around the cushions and arms, we usually cleaned this with a damp cloth. The fire was housed in a black leaded range, which also housed two ovens. A charred black kettle, hung on a hook over the fire. The range was cleaned with black lead polish; a brand called Zebra was universally used, as expected, it came in a black and white stripped tin. It was applied and buffed up using a small brush which got into all the nooks and crannies. Brass candle sticks stood either side of a clock on the mantel shelf. Horse brasses hung on leather straps down each side. The brasses were cleaned at the same time as the range, newspaper was laid on the floor, Brasso was applied, which, when dried was polished off with a clean cloth, an easy job, but messy. The hearth was quarry tiled, often covered in ash from the coal fire. There was always a companion set on the hearth on which hung a poker, brush and small shovel. The hearth was surrounded by a polished wooden or brass fender. A mirror always hung on the wall above the fireplace; we used to stand on the fender to get a view of ourselves in the mirror.In the late fifties and sixties most of these ranges were replaced by tiled fire places. The cleaning was much easier, in many cases the brasses were dumped at the same time, being replaced with smaller, china or porcelain figures which were more suitable.

Once the range was cleaned; we had reached the bottom, nearly finished but not quite. The floor usually covered in Lino or Linoleum, the real poverty stricken had bare floor boards, sometimes painted with a dark brown paint or a brown varnish. The floor, whatever the covering, or lack of, was swept using a
sweeping brush, starting at the front window, ending up with a pile of dust to be deposited in the kitchen. The silly thing was that all the dust and dirt, disturbed by the brush ascended. By the time the floor was mopped, the furniture didn't look like it had been polished. Top to bottom or bottom to top, the outcome was the same either way.

After a good beating and banging against the outside walls, the rugs were ready to be out back into place. Vacuum cleaners weren't available and wouldn't have been any good on those floor coverings. The Bex Bissell carpet brush only came into its own when Axminster carpets became more widely used.

The kitchen was at the back of the house and was a different matter. It was square and had three rooms off it. The pantry, which had a concrete still or slab for cold foods, and shelves around the walls. Everyday plates, bowls and cooking pots were on the shelves, cups hung on the edges of the shelves on hooks. Bottled fruit, pickles and preserves were kept on the top shelf, tinned foods on the bottom; heavy items were housed on the floor.

Next to the pantry was the coal house and was a step down from the kitchen floor. The coalman, literally emptied his one hundred weight sack of coal, straight into this space and the dust went all over the house, thank God he never came on a Saturday. Besides coal, certain implements were kept in the coal house such as a large shovel and a small shovel. The larger of the two, was generally used to put in front of the fire, newspaper was placed over the whole front, this must had created a sort of vacuum because it was used to draw the fire up or get it going. When the paper turned brown and started to ignite, an adult would quickly screw it up and push it up the chimney, fingers crossed that it didn't catch fire. Chimney fires were a common problem, especially if the chimney hadn't been swept. A job usually done by the chimney sweep. A chimney fire was usually spotted by an eagle eyed neighbour who had seen an unusual amount of smoke belching out the top. The small shovel was used to throw slack behind the lumps of coal on the fire. This process was used to make the coal burn longer. A bucket was kept for carrying the coal to the fire, probably the same bucket used for the cleaning.

Whiter Than White.

The third room was the bathroom, it housed a cast iron, white enamelled bath, it stood on small cast iron feet. There was no fancy side, to hide whatever had been pushed underneath. The cast iron boiler in the corner was covered with a large wooden lid; this was used as a table top everyday except Monday. The only other item was a huge square tank, which held hot water, produced by the back boiler situated behind the fire. This was the only source of hot water, so if we needed hot water in the summer, we had to have the fire going. Steam was constantly given off from the hot water tank, making the bathroom damp, dank and musty. Any clothes left lying around for any length of time were ruined by mildew.

The bath was used once a week, on a Saturday night. We were scrubbed and polished ready for the Sabbath, our day of rest and obviously, something to do with cleanliness being next to Godliness. We didn't luxuriate in bubbles; we had a large square block of green Fairy, or yellow Sunlight soap. If you were posh or better off, you would have a bath size block of red Lifebuoy, but it had a strange smell of disinfectant. We didn't have shampoo and conditioner either. Hair was washed with the soap that we used to wash our bodies. It was however, rinsed with diluted vinegar, supposed to make the hair shine and probably keep the lice at bay. If we ever got head lice we were treated with a white lotion called Suleo, it contained DDT. Our hair was soaked in the stuff, it had to be left in all night and washed out the next day, this didn't happen very often, our mother was very handy with a nit comb. The youngest kids got in the bath first and, after being washed and rinsed, out they came, were wrapped in a towel and they would run into the living room, to be dried in front of the fire. The oldest were the last to get into the water, which by this time had a layer of scum on the top, and an even bigger layer around the edge, which stayed put when the water was drained out.

The toilet wasn't in the bathroom, oh no, it was actually out side and was unlit. How ironic, that architects in those days, felt it was more important, to have the coal house inside, and the toilet out side. There was no sink in the bathroom either; the only sink in the house was the one in the kitchen.

There wasn't a lot of room in the kitchen come to think of it, what with five doors and a window, wall space was limited. A table took centre stage, bleached, plain wooden, in the early days, but replaced with a smarter model when Formica was introduced, it was easier to clean too. A gas cooker with four burners, a small oven with a grill above, occupied the space near to the bath room door. This must have been a convenient place, considering that the gas supply served the cooker and the boiler. On a longer stretch of wall was a virtual floor to ceiling, cumbersome wooden cupboard, two long doors at the top, covered a number of shelves, on which were kept packet food and dry groceries. An open shelf divided the top from the bottom and all sorts of things were found on there. I wouldn't say it was a very tidy home, and this type of surface didn't help. Beneath the shelf were two very deep drawers, so much was crammed into these, that it was nigh impossible to find anything. Understandable I guess, since large families tended to occupy these properties, so storage space was at a premium. Two cupboard doors at the bottom hid two very deep shelves, all our shoes, scarves, hats, infact almost all our outdoor attire was kept or rather thrown in there.

As things improved and people became better off, kitchen cabinets became flavour of the day. They were so much smaller, than the big wooden council issue, which they replaced. About five feet high, the top shelves were covered with a sliding glass door. Below that was a pull down Formica area, which acted as a working area. These cabinets were mostly made of Plywood, and came in bright, clean colours, ours was blue and yellow. There were some spectacular bon fires when everyone chopped up their council issue, wooden cupboards, the fortunate thing was that the council never asked for them back.

Whiter Than White.

The kitchen sink, being the only one in the house was used for everything, from washing the dishes, the pots and the pans. Preparing vegetables and other foods, hand washing special clothes such as woollens, and for our personal hygiene, which apart from our Saturday bath was used on a daily basis, there were nine of us altogether, so it was well used. The sink was a white enamel Belfast sink which was quite deep. The draining board on the side was for many years wooden. It had grooves down its length for the water to run back into the sink. It often got very wet, slimy and smelly, eventually; the bottom end would rot away and drop off, the council replacing it when necessary. A fabric or plastic curtain, usually hung around the sink and draining board, creating extra storage space for cleaning products, such as washing powder, soap and vim. Beside the sink was always a bar of soap, ordinary every day stuff, that we used to wash our hands and faces every morning. A tin of Gibbs pink toothpaste was on the window sill usually open, it was too much trouble to put the lid back on. A couple of well worn tooth brushes lay nearby, these were used by anyone inclined to clean their teeth, it was not obligatory. Come to think of it, did Dad use these same brushes for his dentures, perish the thought. The tooth paste was quite a hard pink block in a round tin. The block had to be scrubbed quite a bit, with water and the tooth brush to make it into a paste and usable, no wonder it seemed to last such a long time. Sometimes there was a tin of Swarfega, a soft soap, used mainly for washing oily hands. Garages used to keep it for the mechanics to use at the end of the day.

Until the fifties, the kitchen, pantry and bathroom walls were bare brick, usually covered in gloss paint. A light colour on the top half and a darker colour on the bottom, probably to prevent dirty little hand marks showing. During the fifties the council upgraded and they were all plastered. A red quarry floor covered the kitchen, pantry and bathroom. After being swept out, the floor was scrubbed, using a big block of hard soap and a scrubbing brush. I remember one time; I got too much soap on the tiles, every time I tried to rinse it off with a damp cloth, it just kept soaping up, the soap was lodged in-between the tiles, it took an age that day.

The outside toilet, which consisted of a toilet with a high water cistern, a chain with a long wooden handle at the end, hung down the side. The chain was pulled to flush the toilet. After cleaning the toilet, the floor was mopped and the bucket then emptied into the outside drain which we called a grid.

The last job of all was the front steps. We had three by the front door, a short path led to another four by the front gate. Everybody had steps of some sort and generally they were kept tidy, a case of first impressions perhaps. Some people used red Cardinal, it was hard work but, used on a regular basis, polish on top of polish, didn't take too much effort. Our steps were done with white step stone or donkey stone as some called it; it was a white square block, possibly some sort of calcium. A bucket of warm water, a cloth and a step stone were all that was required. After sweeping the steps down, they were wet, using the cloth which was generally soaking wet, the steps were porous and absorbed water very quickly. The step stone was soaked for a while in the water and, was then rubbed several times over the step, both the rise and the tread. Once a good quantity had been applied, the cloth, tightly wrung out, was used to create a smooth finish. It had to be done in straight lines, right to left, left to right so that it dried with no smudges. Nobody was allowed to put a foot on the steps until they dried, otherwise the imprints would be there for a week. The one doing the cleaning was not exempt and had to climb a wall to get back on the path, which went around the side of the house to the back.

Cleaning finished for another week and we could start to relax. If ever we had any visitors, it was friends from church who came around on Sunday. The house was at its best and we

Whiter Than White.

were all scrubbed up and in our Sunday finery.

RED RAG TO A BULL.

Apart from an annual seaside holiday, which few could afford, and then, only towards the late fifties, early sixties. The annual Sunday school trip, which would take coach loads of us to Milford Common, Rudyard Lake, Ipstones and the like. We all gathered at church and there would be a line of coaches, as many as five or six. Refreshments were loaded, followed by hoards of excited kids; friends and siblings sticking together when allocated seats. There were no rules or regulations and no seatbelts. As many as four children, would be on a seat meant for two, we never minded, just squashed up and in some cases, sat on each others knees.

On arrival at our destination, there would be organised games and a quasi sports competition, when winners would be presented with a prize. At some Point; there was the inevitable bun fight. Loads of sandwiches and cakes prepared and donated by the ladies of the church. It was all washed down with home made lemonade, sometimes, we were lucky enough to get a piece of fruit, and that was a treat. Lucky bags or party bags hadn't been thought of back then. A free day out on a coach, was a bonus for attending Sunday school and certainly wasn't to be sniffed at.

Other venues included Drayton Manor Park, which in those day's was just that, but with a few mechanical rides. I now take my grandchildren and what a difference half a century makes. Alton Towers too, consisted of beautiful gardens and the ruined towers, plenty of grassy areas for picnics and games. Rowing and paddle boats on the lake, man power, being the order of the day, rather than the massive electric powered rides of today.

Mow Cop was another place, situated on the Staffordshire/Cheshire border. It was to my mind a hill with a sort of folly in ruins, which was always known locally, as the old man of mow. I can only imagine this location was popular, because of its association with the Wesley brothers and Methodism, which had very deep roots in that area commonly recognised as the birth place of Methodism. The Wesley brothers were both Anglicans. They formed societies, which they hoped would be incorporated in the Anglican Church. The brothers were called Methodists by those who opposed them and the name stuck. I believe both brothers died Anglicans. It was only after their death, that the Methodist movement came into being.

Occasionally, we had a school trip, mostly the junior and senior schools. This always involved a train journey, Which, in itself was quite an adventure! Because of the layout of the train, the teachers couldn't be everywhere and a group of eight or ten, could be in the carriage without direct supervision. What a ball that was! I remember swinging from the luggage racks above the seats, we pretended to be monkeys and we made a pretty good job of it. Every so often, an adult would look in on us and a head count was done, something that continued on a regular basis throughout the day.

We would walk, snake like, two abreast, in a well behaved manner, we could not let our school down. Eventually we would arrive at the beach, where we spent the rest of the day. The older ones would be allowed the freedom to do a little souvenir shopping, we would be given a time to return and a meeting place. If any child failed to show up or was in effect lost, one of the teachers, had to stay back, until the child was found, they would then catch a later train. There was a 100% return rate, even though on occasions a little late. This trip was the only occasion when some children saw the sea and some, not even then, because the one's whose parents either couldn't or wouldn't pay the fare, had to spend the day in school.

Family day's out, were confined to high days and holidays, since in some form or another money was involved. The potters were lucky, because on our doorstep was a very beautiful attraction known as Trentham gardens. The home of the Dukes of Sutherland. In its heyday, it attracted people from far and wide.

Red Rag To A Bull.

In fact on one occasion, a family from Stoke-on-Trent, were on holiday in Blackpool and during their stay, booked to go on a mystery tour. The joke, was, they ended up in Trentham Gardens, all the way from Blackpool!

The gardens were definitely one up from the park. A visit to the gardens was usually on a bank holiday Monday, sometimes known as wakes Monday. There was an entrance charge and people queued along the frontage, everybody carrying bags of foodstuff and rugs to put on the grass.The mood was always happy, we couldn't wait to get admitted through the turnstiles and hey presto! We were in. It was another world.

A smooth, clean, tarmac driveway on which there was hardly ever any traffic and we were free to run and roam. The lawns were perfectly manicured, the shrubbery lush and thick. The Italian gardens were truly magnificent, as was the gorgeous rose archway, covered for about fifty yards, in a beautiful pink, seven sisters climbing rose.Walking through there, was like walking into a wonderland.

There was an enormous lake, with all sorts of sailing craft, rowing boats, paddle boats and a large passenger carrying boat. For an extra charge, we would sometimes but not always have a trip. We would be allowed to queue on the jetty and take our turn to board the boat. It was sometimes a long wait, but once on, we were as happy as if we were doing a world cruise on a P & O liner. Sadly, the trip was over all too soon, happily the memories out lasted the trip.

Then there was the famous train, boarded at a proper station, we would take our seats and the conductor would walk, from one end to the other, collecting our fare. Safely on board, the green flag was raised, the whistle blew and off we went. The steam choo, chooing, as we wended our way, on a fantastic journey through the woods, so cooling, on a hot summer's day.

Our destination was usually the wonderful open air swimming pool. That was a dream on a hot day, but, I can't ever remember being able to swim, there never seemed enough room, because, there were so many people in the pool. There couldn't have been any restriction on numbers and the attendants, attired in crisp white shirt or blouse, flannels or skirt and white plimsolls or pumps as we called them, only seemed concerned, with the management of the changing rooms. These were at one end of the pool, male one side, and female the other and no meeting in the middle! To one side of the pool was a tiered wooden stand for spectators. The other two sides, were grassy banks where there was lots of sunbathing and picnicking.

Towards the end of the day, we would go around collecting all the returnable glass bottles, that had been left lying around and return them to the cafeteria, where we collected all the deposits, we could make a small fortune. I cannot understand, when people had so little, how they could be so careless. We were brought up to look after the pennies and the pounds will look after themselves, how true. There were other anecdotes such as, pay as you go, if you can't pay, don't go. If you can't afford to pay for it, you can't afford to have it. Neither lender nor borrower be and owe no man, no mention of woman!! Principles, which would not go amiss in the twenty first century.

Barlaston Downs was a great place and a day out often involved extended family, as we would be joined by aunties, uncles and cousins. It was countryside, pure and simple and we would always be accompanied by adults. The downs were accessed by legally crossing farmer's fields. A herd of cows often had to be negotiated and occasionally, it would be the bull. On one occasion, it was the bull and I was wearing a red dress. The colour red was said to antagonise a bull, hence the saying, red rag to a bull. In order to get past, my mother put me underneath her skirt and led me in front of her, until we were well out of sight.

We always took food and there was a small isolated farm cottage that did pots of tea and hot water for a few pence. There was one area that was particularly beautiful, the grass was soft and short almost as if it was mowed and beside was a crystal clear stream. We always occupied this spot. The downs were never crowded, all day could be spent, only ever seeing perhaps half a dozen other families. Here we would play, paddle in the freezing stream and picnic.

Often, we would venture out into bluebell wood, a true favourite. On one occasion, an aunt that had joined us for the day almost cut the end off her finger, picking bluebells. We were told always to pull them from the base, and we carried armfuls home, the perfume pervading the house for days, reminding us of our day in the country. The beauty of the woods was awesome, and I regret, not leaving the blooms for others to enjoy. Seen very differently through older eyes and mature mind, an understanding of the verse, take nothing but memories, leave nothing but footprints, kill nothing but time.

Rudyard Lake was another haunt, situated near to Leek. As its name suggests, it was a huge lake, possibly man made. There were sailing craft of various types and other amusements and activities on the shore line. It was accessed by bus, entry was free but obviously, all the facilities carried a charge.

Like most families in the forties and fifties we didn't own a car. My father was very friendly with a butcher in Liverpool Road, Stoke. A Hughie Wainwright as I recall, a lovely unpretentious family. They owned a really super, big, Riley car. My father would do some building work for them on occasions and in return, besides payment, would get a loan of the car. On those days we would go further afield. We marvelled at the shiny, polished wooden dashboard and the plush leather upholstery. All us kids would be on the back seat, sitting on each others knees. Did we feel like royalty? you bet, Chester Zoo, here we come.

THE GENERATION GAP.

Extended families were common, before, during and for sometime after the Second World War. Young married couples would rent a room in a house, preferably with one or other of their parents. This was not always possible, a married older sibling could already be occupying a room in the family home, or there could be many younger siblings still to be accommodated. Working class people certainly didn't own houses and whole houses for rent were scarce and unaffordable, so, would be shared by a few families renting one or two rooms.

By far the best option was to get on the council house waiting list. The climb to the top of the list was on a points system, much as it is today. Points were awarded for various reasons, number one being the extent of overcrowding in a property, which would have been considered a public health issue. Other points would have been the length of time married and importantly, most points given for the number of children of the marriage. Not unlike today, except that most on the waiting list now are single and for reasons possibly attributable to the change in our society and social structure, produce the offspring in order to get to the top.

After the war, as after all conflicts, when the men returned home there was the inevitable baby boom and people needed to be accommodated. For this reason the councils had to act quickly and a house building programme was implemented. Some properties were prefabricated structures and could be erected in a matter of days. They were basically concrete and metal and were meant to last only a few years. In some localities they called these areas tin towns for obvious reasons. Considering the expected short longevity of these properties, how amazing that they still stand, occupied and looking quite decent some sixty odd years later.

The working and social set up meant that we were very close to our extended family, much as it still is in the eastern part of our globe. Wherever we were, we knew someone. Grandma's house in particular was a haven and grand kids much loved and spoiled. I never knew my maternal grandmother; she died very young, leaving six children, two of whom were under school age. My maternal grandfather remarried some time later, an old friend who was a childless widow. She became a good mother to the young ones and a good grandmother. The general history of the distaff side of the family is patchy, probably due to the circumstances already described. We always went to this grandparent's home for Sunday lunch. I and several of my siblings, after attending morning Sunday school, would catch the bus to Hartshill church, alight and

The Generation Gap.

walk down Queens road, past the cemetery to our grandparents home in Penkhull. In autumn the many trees around that cemetery area would shed their leaves and we would be knee deep, kicking the leaves ahead as we walked. It was something we enjoyed and even looked forward to.

Once there, the smell of the oven met our nostrils and our bellies ached. On most Sunday mornings Dougie the farmer would arrive on a horse drawn trap affair, with the milk churns on board. After delivering the required amount of milk to anyone who approached him with a suitable receptacle, preferably a jug, all the neighbourhood kids, us included, would jump on board for a free ride back to the farm, the downside was, we had to walk back. By which time the lunch was ready to be served and we would take our allocated places at the table, under the very watchful eye of granddad. A stickler for manners and rules which had to be obeyed. Prayers were said, leaving the table without being excused was a definite no, no. Talking at the table was not allowed and cutlery had to be used correctly.

Behind their house was agricultural land, we would go through the gate, onto the field and help with the haymaking. A two pronged pitch fork for anyone with the strength to lift a load of hay and throw it on to the truck. Over the far side of the field was a stream and at certain times of the year we would harvest water cress which was in plentiful supply and free to anyone who wished to get their feet wet.

Once I started my general nurse training, I would often visit my grandparents. A quick hop past childrens ward, through the cow field, over the fence and I was there. Always, during a split shift, when I would be off duty from 2pm to 5pm. I became close to my grandfather during this time. He would often prepare some lunch for me. In the summer, I would sunbathe on the back lawn and in winter, I would rest on the settee in front of a lovely coal fire. At 4pm I would get a little nudge which roused me from my rest, informing me of the time and that my tea was ready. Sometimes, I would meet him at his local, The Terrace Inn where he played cribbage. His face lit up as I made my entrance in my uniform complete with my outdoor cape. He was so proud and always introduced me to his mates. Sadly he died six months before I qualified. I missed him for many a while afterwards.

The falstaff side of the family was different, though my grandfather had died before I was born; our knowledge of the family was quite extensive from our wonderful grandma. Knowledge derived from skeletons jumping out of cupboards rather than remaining locked away. We heard about members of the family that had to get married, my grandma found it amusing that they had even announced the birth of a 9lb premature baby in the local paper. Our great grandfather on granddads side was quite a character and according to all accounts was not too pleasant. Extremely well self educated, was at the turn of the century a well known poet and writer and did infact have several works published.

Grandmas side of the family were all fairly well off and all owned a business of some sort or another. My great Grandmother had a small mixed business, grocery and green grocery down the basin, which was a part of the canal system in Stoke. I remember as a small child going to her shop. She was so strict and intimidating, wore black from head to toe, literally, except for a very beautiful, white starched apron trimmed with lace. The lavvy was down the yard and they used gas lights. She had a lovely figurine which stood on a black plinth under a huge glass dome. The living area was very dark due to net curtains and heavy drapes at the window. A round table took centre place and was covered in a dark green chenille type cover. A black leaded range covered the chimney breast. A pegged rug lay in front of the tiled hearth which was surrounded by a highly polished brass fender. A great uncle had a cobblers shop in Fenton, he was known for his misery. He had lost his only child a son, killed in action in the Second World War, so maybe this accounted for his unpleasant attitude. A great aunt kept Grove fisheries in Heron Cross for many years.

My paternal grandparents had a very big business in Granville Street. It was a property of some considerable size, owned I believe by a brewery. A mixed grocery and greengrocery occupied a large area. Separate to this was the out house or off licence where ale was sold by the pint or whatever but certainly not by the litre. This was for consumption off the premises usually in the customer's home. At the back was a bakery of some considerable size. A couple of the Beckett daughters worked in the bakery alongside my grandfather. This would be his job before he went to his main employment which was in the wagon repair shop at Sneyd colliery. The hours they put in were long and arduous, starting with the bakery at 5am and finishing with the closure of the off licence at 10pm. Sunday was very definitely a much needed day of rest. My grandmother was in the position of having daily help and we always knew this lady as aunty Maud, it was many years later when we realized that she was no relation.

My grandmother produced three children, two boys and a girl. The oldest son was to become my father. As a child he was spoiled rotten. He became quite an accomplished pianist, often

The Generation Gap.

playing by ear. This talent was encouraged and he was the proud owner of a beautiful baby grand piano which stood in the music room. He also had a twelve bore shot gun. My grandma often related the story, that one day her younger son was upstairs when she heard the gun go off. She went cold with the thought that he might have shot himself and gingerly ventured up the stairs, dreading the scene that awaited. To her joy and surprise he was alive and well. He had put the barrel of the gun into the feather bed before pulling the trigger. Feathers were everywhere, even pinned to the door with shot. At some point, my father wanted a bicycle. My grandfather took him to Ron Whittakers, a well known cycle shop in Liverpool road Stoke. He duly chose the bike, but wanted a few extras. Grandfather was known to the owner, so, left him to sort Dad out with the promise of settling up later. Grandma was just enjoying a tea break as he walked through the gate, pushing his bike adorned with saddle bag, lights and mirrors. She almost choked on her tea as she exclaimed "what's he got, a bloody Morgan"? Morgan's being the very exclusive hand made cars which they are to this day.

She kept us kids amused with her tales from the past. Many years later, her stays at my home were frequent and my two kids would always end up in her bed in the mornings as she regaled them with tales from the past.

The Generation Gap.

Now, my grandchildren end up in my bed for a cuddle and guess what-tell us the stories your grandma told you about the past, will it continue for more generations. It seems the bigger the age gap, the stronger the bond.

My grandfather had died at the age of 44years. As a child I heard a lot about him and everyone spoke well. He was kindly and generous, feeding the Wickliffe bible college trekkers as they came to preach in our area. He always made sure that his poorer neighbours with large families had warm food, often in the shape of a huge meat and potato pie. Being in business meant that they were well placed and I guess, quite well off in comparison to some. One neighbour came to the shop and asked grandma if he could borrow granddads bowler hat, he had to attend a funeral. Of course, was the reply, I'll get it for thee. The bowler was duly produced and grandma explained that if necessary, it could be made smaller by putting some newspaper inside the leather facing. When granddad returned, he was told, that's ok he said but, did you take the £20 notes from inside the leather facing? Grandma went weak at the knees. She needn't have worried, the bowler was returned intact.

Well before the war, things changed and became very difficult. With the death of her husband, she was left to manage a huge business and three children, just about in their teens. Her generous nature was not easily changed and during the war years found it hard to refuse people food on tick or credit. Her own financial situation was becoming precarious and during the war she took a second job at Rolls Royce in the Basin, working on aeroplane engines for the war effort. Much of her customer's debt was never repaid and she found it hard to manage two jobs and settle her own financial obligations. She gave up the business and moved to a rented property, a modest three bedroom family home, only a few houses from where we lived. She continued to work and after the war, took a job in a plastics factory called Teddy Toys. This place produced plastic garments, grandma was not averse to bringing home the plastic off cuts which ensured that we always had lots of colourful plastic hair ribbons. She was determined never to go bankrupt; she worked for many years to avoid this disgrace and was successful. She owed no one, but was poor to the end with a heart of gold.

Living so near meant that we saw her daily and although her means were limited, it was the place where a treat was guaranteed. If we were in trouble at home, it was grandma to whom we ran. There were times when several of us, as we got older actually spent some time living there, when things got difficult at home. No such luxury for many of today's youngsters, who, if lucky end up in a hostel if not, on the street with a board, hungry and homeless, is that progress?

Grandma's was always warm and welcoming. The toilet, which had a very well scrubbed, clean, warm wooden seat, was down the yard. We would have to pass it on our way to the back door, which was our usual entry, the door never being locked. Who's there, grandma would call if she happened to be in the toilet as we passed, we would reply. There was a tiny hole in the toilet door through which a small shaft of light illuminated the otherwise dark closet. The hole was also just big enough for a small finger to be poked through it, the finger getting a tender, loving wiggle from the inside. Behind the lavvy was a disused out house, where chickens had once been kept. Unfortunately, they appeared to attract mice and grandma was terrified of the little pests, so the chickens had to go. The yard was more practical than pretty. Staffordshire blue brick covered the yard from wall to wall; the bricks were brushed and washed weekly. The walls surrounding the yard had an annual coat of lime wash or distemper which dried white and covered the walls up to the first floor window sills.

Indoors, there was always a glowing fire in the polished black leaded range. A big wire toasting fork hung at the side. Grandma would

The Generation Gap.

sit with a slice of bread as thick as a door step, placed on the prongs at the end of the fork and toasted in front of the fire. Once cooked, it would be smothered in dripping, pure animal fat with a sort of very tasty brown meaty jelly at the bottom of the pot, everybody wanted the jelly. The toast, once covered in dripping would be liberally sprinkled with salt and downed with a cup of tea. I many a time saw Grandma cook a rasher of bacon in the same way. There was always a kettle on the boil, sometimes a pot of stew on the go and often a pie in the oven. These enormous ranges were multi purpose and were used to the full. Home baking and home cooking was the norm.The table which was square with one side placed against the wall, was always laid or set, with sugar, milk and a freshly made pie. Grandma's pies were legendary and contained only fresh fruit, gooseberries, rhubarb, apple, blackberries and bilberries, the latter being my favourites, though they seem not to be available these days. It was taken for granted that when ever we walked in we would get a piece of tart. We never had to ask and if we did, it was never denied.

As we got older, domestic science in school was compulsory. We had to take money to school to pay for the ingredients of whatever we were cooking that day. The end result would then be taken home. Mother was never very happy to give us the money, maybe she

The Generation Gap.

was short. In spite of grandma being in the same position, she would be the one we would ask. Mum expected the contents of the dish, never the less. If mum wouldn't buy our school photos, grandma would. She never liked the idea that we might be looked down upon for returning them to school. That said, seven lots of photos wouldn't come cheap and it is possible that mum just couldn't afford these things.The same went for fund raising items.

At least once a year, we would all be given about 10 Phul Nana scent cards, which we had to sell for school funds. They were normally placed among clothes; I suppose scented clothes hid some of the obvious B.O. If mum couldn't or wouldn't buy, grandma always would, not that she needed them any more than anyone else.There is no use for such cards these days and they can only be found in museums of sorts.

We never had pocket money but if ever we wanted a few sweets or a three penny bit for the bug run, which was the common term for the cinema, to watch the Saturday afternoon matinee. Mother was never to know, she strongly disapproved of the pictures, even a cowboy film starring Roy Rogers and his horse Trigger. Cigarette smoking was widespread and as kids we would buy imitation packets of sweet cigarettes. They were basically a stick of hard icing with a red tip at one end, we would pretend to smoke and felt quite grown up. The box itself was a miniature of the real thing. The packets often contained what we called cigarette cards. These were often of well known sports personalities or film stars, the likes of, Betty Grable, Doris Day, and Clarke Gable. It was always a dream to see these idols on the screen. Saturday afternoon was the only chance we had to sneak off.

In her middle age, grandma seemed to lose the religion she once held dear. Maybe due to the unfortunate events that had overtaken her in recent years. She remained a wonderful humanist with a big heart which was in the right place. This situation often conflicted with mother who was religious to the end. If mother fell out with grandmother for any reason, she kept us away; we were not allowed any contact. She only lived eight houses away from us and we had to pass her door. Etched deep in my memory were the Sunday afternoons, on our way to Sunday school. There would be four or five of us, grandma knew exactly what time we would be passing her gate, she would stand there in order to see us. My mother would stand at our gate in order to check that we didn't disobey her instructions. We had to walk past grandma without as much a glance. How broken hearted she must have been, as I grew older my heart ached for her and it drew us closer. How do you reconcile sending children to church to be taught right from wrong, about loving our neighbours, at the

The Generation Gap.

same time, in practice, instilling the opposite and, in the process denying the kids, the love, warmth and kindness of a dear grandmother. My aunt and uncle never married and lived with grandma. They enjoyed a different lifestyle to ours; they danced together, often travelling to venues such as Belle Vue in Manchester for dancing competitions. They often competed and won, especially in the jive and the jitterbug and on that circuit became quite well known. I loved to watch, envious of their ease of movement, rhythm and timing. Our
religious upbringing denied us the opportunity to dance, it was considered worldly. Even now I sit in the back ground while others enjoy the floor. Grandma's house was full of music and it was there that I developed a love of classical music. She lived to the ripe old age of 85 years. The things she taught me have lasted my life time, will the circle continue?

NO WINNERS.

Religion was the order of the day, whether or not that religion was Christianity is to me debateable. Whatever it was, it was practised by the majority of the population. It is said that in times of need and hardship, people turn to God. The affluence of today has rendered many churches empty and a fair number succumbing to dereliction. The main survivors being the Roman Catholic Church and the Church of England. Both being very rich by one means or another, the Church of England, reputed to be one of the biggest land and property owners in the country. In some communities the Church of England was too high and more akin to Rome. This idea even extended to the common market and the Treaty of Rome. It was firmly believed that we would end up governed by the Vatican.

Our family erred on the side of the evangelicals, whose teaching and fellowship seemed more appealing to the working classes. There were many small Churches or missions that catered for this large group of people, alongside the Baptists,Pentecostals and other independent groups including the Methodists and Weslyan Methodists. North of Stoke is a hillock called Mow Cop, on which stand the ruined remains of a monument, known locally as the old man of Mow. This area seemed to attract religious activity. I recall my father talking about Gypsy Smith, who not only preached but also wrote some great music and hymns. It is also thought to be the home of Methodism and certainly, John Wesley and his brother Charles are reputed to have delivered some very powerful sermons from that spot. John Wesley was not a Methodist. He formed societies which he wanted to be associated within the Anglican Church. The word Methodist was used in a derogatory manner towards the Wesley brothers by those who opposed them. However, the word stuck, John Wesley died an Anglican and it was only after his death that the Methodist movement came into being.

My mother was saved during the war years, when my father was still fighting abroad. He was a dispatch rider, carrying messages to the front line in North Africa. His war service ended in Sicily following the "march" through Italy. He returned to a very different wife, from a regular dancer and cinema goer to a religious, pious, church attendee. Although he attended church, even playing the organ and piano at times, he never became a fully fledged member. This was due to his life long smoking habit, which was considered a sin. The church we attended being very strict. It started life as a tin mission, being built by the garage and haulage family, the Becketts. It was for a long time known as Becketts Mission in spite of being allied to denominations such as the Calvary Holiness Mission, the International

No Winners.

Holiness Mission and in the fifties becoming the Church of the Nazarene, which was and still is very big in parts of America and the Caribbean.

In the middle of the twentieth century, church attendance was still quite high; in some areas these churches are not now able to support a Minister or Pastor as they were called. Our early years were dominated by the church and it was the only activity besides school that was allowed. Everything that wasn't church based was worldly and sinful and had no place in our extra curricular activities.

Church was our life and as we grew older our attendance increased. Five times on a Sunday, this would consist of morning Sunday school followed by morning service. After lunch we would be off again to afternoon Sunday school. During this time our parents would retire to their bed for an afternoon kip or so we thought. Were we sent to Sunday school for our spiritual well being or for their conjugal rights to be enjoyed in peace and quiet? In spite of the well intentioned former, I suspect the latter. We returned home in silence and the older of us would start to prepare Sunday tea, paste or spam sandwich followed by half a preserved peach or pear, jelly and custard occasionally carnation milk. A tidy up was followed by Evening service and then the youth group, which was a service especially for the young people and generally called the Y.P.group. This would take place in the home of one of the church members, the venue rotating on a voluntary basis. This was the social side of church attendance. We would enjoy fellowship and food, the latter at times being the attraction.

Our church activities continued apace throughout the week. Tuesday night was bible study, Wednesday night was prayer meeting, and Thursday night was the Y.P. meeting. The Saturday night fellowship meeting was replaced once a month by the missionary meeting when we learned of the wonderful work our missionaries were doing, saving the souls of our starving brothers and sisters, mostly in the African and South American continents. This practice, though tried was not so successful in Asia, since those societies had a very strong religious base. It was Swami Vivekananda a Hindu monk, who was given three minutes to speak at a religious convention in Chicago in 1893, said, "you send missionaries to our country to feed their souls, they have religion enough, give them bread for their stomachs". His address lasted approximately fifteen days.

In a sense we became missionaries in our own society and locality. The Y.P. would often go up to Hanley on a Saturday night to the Tabernacle which we called The Cathedral, on

No Winners.

Town Road. It was quite a huge church and would be full to the gunnels with young people from various churches around the potteries; it was the weekly Youth for Christ meeting. The atmosphere was electric; we sang our hearts out raising the roof, especially during the hymn Christ for me which we adopted as our anthem.

During the fifties we had visits from a number of evangelists such as Eric Hutchins and the renowned Billy Graham. Meetings called crusades were held across the country. In Stoke-on-Trent they were held in the Victoria Hall. These meetings were highly charged and emotional, the climax was the call to penitence. During the very quiet solemn hymn called Jesus I Come, the evangelist would invite all those wishing to give their hearts and lives to the Lord Jesus Christ to come forward. Many people such as myself had been trained as councillors. We would make our way down and position ourselves behind or at the side of the penitent. At the end of the service we would lead them to a quiet area where the commitment that they had made would be explained quoting from the scriptures. They were invited to attend local churches where their faith could be reinforced and they could enjoy the fellowship of like minded people.

This religion being enforced, we knew no other life. Week in, week out the wages of sin were hammered into our conscience as the pastor thumped the pulpit, warning us of impending damnation in the form of fire and brimstone. The pitchfork and the man with the two red horns, mocking the thousands, squirming and pleading for salvation in the pit that was hell.

Dancing was banned, considered worldly. As I grew older and after marriage started to attend various functions, I envied my contemporaries, gliding over the floor with such ease and enjoyment. I would sit on the side lines and dream. A dream that would never become reality, since the rigors of older age and the psychological indoctrination in my early life put paid to that. The cinema was considered no better, the stars of the silver screen were no good, loose women or fornicators. The principle was, that by paying to see them act, was tantamount to encouraging their sinful lifestyle. Until the sixties cinema's were in abundance and probably had a bigger attendance than the churches. The Majestic, Gaumont, Odeon and the Dannilo were the bigger names but there were numerous others, two or three in a town and often called the bug run, go in walking, come out riding, they obviously had a reputation for not being too clean. To adorn oneself was frowned upon as not being Godly, so make up was out of the question. In my late teens I sometimes bought a little discreet make up but as soon as it was discovered it went straight to the back of the fire. We would employ the ways and means act until we were old enough and hopefully wise enough to make our own decisions.

During the forties and fifties a few of our relatives on the distaff side were involved with the communist party. As kids we were taken to tea parties put on by the communist party, whether my mother was aware that we were attending a party connected to a political organisation is not known. During the event we would be treated to a film show, explaining the wonderful life the children of Russia enjoyed, in their red and white outfits with happy smiling faces, giving the impression of the freedom that they enjoyed. Many years later the truth became clear and this was nothing more than communist propaganda. The indoctrination was opportunity and equality for all. A quasi religious movement, nationalism versus communism, good versus evil. One of the great expounders of communism, Karl Marx, wrote that religion was the opium of the masses, what better way to put it. In many parts of the world it is used as a weapon, to keep the masses quiet and happy.

As in all religions fear played a great part, the communist preaching was the bomb and in particular the nuclear bomb. The terrible suffering that would be inflicted upon the human race and worse still was the impending extinction of mankind and the total destruction of our planet, which was as sure to happen as day follows night. I was greatly affected. I had a great love for my fellow man and of course my own mortality was important. I felt compelled to write to our then M.P. Ellis Smith, imploring him to do all in his power to convince the government of the day to halt this impending disaster.

Events decades later, with the almost total break up of the Soviet Empire did the true reality of the communist system become evident. During the fifties, whichever route was taken, annihilation was inevitable. Either way you'd had it, if the bomb didn't get you then hell fire and damnation would.

NEVER HAD IT SO GOOD.

The years of war, austerity and poverty were starting to become a distant memory. Living standards started to improve, aided by full employment. Jobs were certainly plentiful, and it was true, that you could walk out of one job today and into another tomorrow. I was fortunate enough to stay in education until I was in my eighteenth year, but school leavers even at fifteen could literally take their pick of vocational, clerical or manual work.

It was during the fifties, that mothers started to spend more time at home. Understandably, the end of the war brought with it the inevitable baby boom. These new citizens would require education, jobs and housing within a couple of decades. Ammunition factories either closed or reduced production and the land was again worked by the men. Servicemen, returning after demobilisation were found jobs mostly in the construction industry which was to enjoy many boom years.

Though wages were relatively low, spending power increased. The world appeared to have hit the jackpot. Money was available and that fuelled the demand for the products, produced by our industries, up and down the country, from textiles, steel and pottery to ship building, locomotives and aero engines. The pits worked flat out to supply the coal needed to produce the energy that all these industries required.

Never Had It So Good.

More spending power meant that household commodities, including furniture and kitchen utensils such as pressure cookers, once out of reach became affordable. By necessity, these and many other goods would be transported from place of manufacture, eventually, to retail outlets. It was around this time, that ordinary people started to own cars.

The need for a better road infrastructure was evident and 1957 saw the opening of the M1 and M6. Fantastic in their heyday, but a gross miscalculation of the number of vehicles plying these major arteries six decades later, now sees them vastly overcrowded, and often at snails pace or standstill due to the volume of traffic.

Dr Beeching the then government minister for transport, had a fantastic brainwave, we get everyone onto the roads, and close most of the rail network. The loop lines as they were called were common to most cities, Stoke-on-Trent being no different. The trains called at every town and many places in-between. In Fenton we had two stations, Fenton which stood at the end of Church Street, almost bordering heron cross, and Fenton Manor which stood on the corner of Manor Street and Victoria Road. How useful, would these wonderful lines be today, especially in the fight against global warming. The tracks were removed and melted down, the land either built on, or, in some cases used as cycle tracks, more especially as cycling has become more popular towards the end of the twentieth century. The stations were sold to individuals, who converted them into beautiful living accommodation.

It was during this time, that the then Prime Minister, Harold Macmillan, was quoted as telling the nation, "you have never had it so good".The government of the day, wanted the ability to use some of new found money and in 1956, came up with the ingenious "ERNIE", which was premium bonds, exactly the same today, except, that the minimum investment then was £1 as compared to £5 today. The value of the prizes has also increased. This was the start of savings for many ordinary folk, who had never had as much as a bank account.

In Stoke-on-Trent, the main areas of employment were in the pits and these were plentiful. The pits not only supplied coal for domestic use, it was not until the late sixties, early seventies, when new build homes had central heating, usually gas fired. Something certainly not enjoyed by the majority, for two to three decades after that, when older properties were converted. The Local coal supported the electric power stations and fired such places as Shelton Bar, a huge steel

Never Had It So Good.

foundry; the sky was always red over Shelton Bar as the furnaces fired twenty four hours a day, seven days a week. The other major area of employment was in the manufacture of china and porcelain. Well known names such as Wedgwood, Minton, Spode and Doulton, which all produced either very fine china or specialist pieces, there were hundreds more producing everyday ware. These factories were known locally as pot banks, and they could be found on almost every other street. The skyline of Stoke-on-Trent from every direction was hundreds of bottle ovens. That was if the skyline could be viewed through the thick smoke that belched out day and night.

During times of natural fog, the prevailing smoky atmosphere added greatly to a situation which became known as smog, a pea souper it was called. Public transport would be suspended, the only way to and from work was by foot, and you literally couldn't see the curb of the pavement beneath your feet. The clean air act, put paid to many of these ovens, and electric kilns were brought into use. It also made a difference to ordinary households who were forced to use smokeless fuel. The clean air act was a success, it greatly reduced the prevalence of cardio-respiratory problems associated with this type of environment.

This period also saw the demise of the black leaded ranges, often situated in living rooms, and housed the fire and ovens. A huge hook supported the smoked black kettle that hung over the fire to boil. The ranges were replaced by tiled fire surrounds, the in thing of the day. The council, responsible for replacing the ones in council owned property. This project, naturally took some time, and the council were inundated by tenants who couldn't wait to go modern. Owner occupiers, the better off had a fancier affair, on which a few more nic nacs could be displayed.

Television was available to the few that could afford it. Like everything else new on the market, they command a high price, which decreases with supply and demand. In no time at all they were being mass produced. Those who couldn't afford to buy outright could rent, and one of the first companies in this field was Reddifusion. They did the lot, put up the aerial and installed the television. There were only two or three channels and programmes, which were then in black and white, were limited to a few hours a day.

In 1952, the announcement, that our beloved King George VI had died, saddened us all. He appeared a humble compassionate monarch and was much admired. For the first time ever, a coronation was to be televised. This was to be the coronation of Queen Elizabeth the second, she was young and beautiful and we were in awe of her. We had followed the lives of

Never Had It So Good.

the young princesses, Elizabeth and her younger sister Margaret in newspaper articles. The spectacle of coronation on television was too good to miss and one or two splashed out on a set. The cabinets, mostly wooden were enormous, the top third housed the screen which measured about 6-8 inches. Our local fish and chip shop proprietor, became the proud owner of one of these specimens.

On the day of the coronation, as expected, the street parties were well in evidence, and the homes where a television existed, became mini cinemas for the day. The world and his wife finding space to watch the event on screen. How wonderful it was, the beautifully embellished, horse drawn, golden coach, carrying a real live princess to be crowned queen. We knew it was golden, because the commentary of Richard Dimbleby was explicit and we believed him. Colour was not available, we saw everything in black and white. This coach was followed, by a procession of horse drawn carriage, after horse drawn carriage, carrying members of our royal family and foreign royal families. Members of the aristocracy, lords, ladies and special guests. Anybody who was anybody, was there in all their finery. The solemnity of the occasion, and the jewels used solely for the coronation as in the crown, orb and sceptre were awesome, a memory to last a lifetime. As if to compliment the day,news came through, that a team of climbers, headed by Hillary,Hunt and Tensing, had for the first time conquered the highest mountain in the world, Mount Everest. They had infact, spent some time training for this successful attempt in Trefan, Snowdonia, North Wales. This event excited us all, and when it was eventually screened at the local cinemas, the queues went on forever and there were full houses day after day. Things were looking up and we all wanted to be a part of it.

Communities started to change, as councils built huge council housing estates on the edge of towns, almost on greenbelt land, which surrounded the city. Families were at last able to have their own accommodation, many moving out of homes, that had housed two, or in some cases three families.Characters, that had been familiar in the close knit communities started to disappear, people like Friday night Fred, a faceless character, only known by his nickname, so called, because, if ever there was a house burglary, it would be on a Friday night. The most obvious, since Friday was pay day and in those days, it was handed out in pounds, shillings and pence.The culprit would be Fred, who was reckoned to wear plimsolls or pumps, in order to avoid detection, or to enable a quick exit, if there was the slightest chance of being caught. Old man Piggott, a lovable old rogue, who professed to always, having a very good Christmas in the nick. This was ensured, by his being arrested for drunken and disorderly behaviour, a day or so before. As kids, we would watch out for Mrs Nick Nock, a colourful character, reckoned to be a bargee from the canal basin. She always rode a sit up and beg bicycle, with a sturdy whicker basket on the front. Rouged cheeks, red lipstick and seemingly endless jewellery adorned her. She always wore a hat, which was decorated with lots of fruit and flowers, much like Carmen Miranda. She attended the solicitor's office, which was almost opposite to our house. Whether we saw her arrive, or knew she was there by the presence of her bicycle, we would anxiously await her departure, out of sheer curiosity and, the fact that we found her demeanour quite entertaining.

A middle aged Down's syndrome man, would always be around the Campbell Place area of Stoke. He thought he was a bus inspector, and would stand at the head of the queue, marshalling the awaiting passengers onto the bus, instructing everyone to hurry up. He was so regular, that he became personally known to many pot bank workers queuing for the bus, to return home at the end of the day. In any event, he was either acknowledged, or ignored, but never as far as I am aware, abused. People were more tolerant of the disabled, possibly because, there was so few about, not because they didn't exist, they did. Facilities to determine an abnormal foetus during pregnancy were not available. An abnormality wouldn't be evident until the child was born or a few months into it's life. Many would die, at or shortly after birth, due to the lack of technical facilities which are available now. Sadly, the very disabled of those that survived would be assigned to institutions, in some cases abandoned, and would spend their whole lives being cared for in a fashion, but never knowing the love and support of a family. State help in the home wasn't an option.

The dissemination of the populace meant that transport was an important part of one's existence. Bus stops were strategically placed, and only on main routes, back streets weren't served by the buses then. The bus stops consisted of a metal pole with a flag like request sign at the top end. No shelter was provided, and a queue would form, whatever the weather. The person nearest the pole was the head off the queue and took precedence over the ones behind. At busy times, buses, though frequent would just fly by full, and that means full to bursting, as many standing as sitting, often one bus following another. Sometimes they would stop but only allow one or two on board. By the time one arrived with space available, if the weather was bad, you could literally be soaked to the skin, an uncomfortable position to be in for the rest of the day, either at work or school. There was no place to shelter, and it was important to keep your place in the queue. We got used to the clothes drying on our backs. People using the buses, which was virtually everyone, were much more amiable and considerate. Seats didn't have to be labelled for use by disabled, the elderly or people with children as they are now. A younger person would always give up their seat for an elder, children sat on parents knees. Men always gave up their seat, for a woman of whatever age. Choice of seat wasn't always available, and it wasn't unknown for a man to sit beside a young woman and try putting his hand up her skirt, knowing that on a full bus, she wouldn't want to make a scene. The hand would usually be lifted and placed on his thigh; dirty old men were around then too. If she did protest, you can be sure that he would be hounded off the bus by the other passengers, especially the men. Sunday saw a limited service; it was after all, Gods day, a day of rest. The only people, who worked, were the ones whose factories never closed down, or members of the emergency services. I was one of the latter. The only bus available to us, I had to be on duty at 7-30am, was the Michelin bus which left at 6-30am. It didn't stop at the usual bus stops, so a walk up to the chemist on Fenton High Street was necessary, and you had to be there in good time to get on otherwise, it was a run into Stoke and hope to get another bus from there.

Never Has It So Good.

We were led to believe, that the Second World War, was the war to end all wars, not so unfortunately. Military personnel, have been involved in wars and skirmishes, on a regular basis ever since. Korea, Yemen, Kenya, Northern Ireland, Falklands and as now, Afghanistan and Iraq. The scariest for me was in 1956, the Suez crisis, caused by the decision of Colonel Abdul Nasser to nationalise the Suez Canal. The British government weren't having any of that, and so started to rally the troops. My father duly received his call up papers, as it happened, it was over very quickly and he didn't have to go. Being demobilised wasn't necessarily the end of one's military service; a call up could come at any time for males of a certain age. However, most conflicts involved young men doing their national service. Two years in one of the services, Army, Navy or Air force was compulsory at the age of eighteen, twenty one for any one doing an apprenticeship. I absolutely dreaded, any of my brothers having to go away, a constant prayer to keep them at home. They were spared, my prayers answered; National Service was abolished in 1959. From then on, the services were manned by regular servicemen, who signed up for however many years by choice. This method operates to this day and, quite successfully.

During the fifties, most of the working population began to feel the benefits of the health service, since it's inception in 1948. Prior to the nationalisation of the health service, institutions and hospitals existed. Some were work houses, where homeless and destitute people lived and worked. They were a desperate last resort, where families were split up, wives separated from husbands and children separated from parents, some for the rest of their lives. The work was back breaking and no one was spared, not even the kids. The food was of poor quality and meagre and the accommodation bleak and bare. Hospitals were usually funded by wealthy industrialists for the benefit of the working classes, many of who made contributions to the hospital via a voluntary deduction from their wage packet. This enabled them and their families, free treatment, accessed by a letter of authority from their employer. This covered all areas of hospital treatment including maternity services. Family Doctors, later to become General Practitioners, were a separate entity and were paid for on a weekly basis. A collector would call on all families registered and collect the financial contributions. It was also not unknown, for family doctors to accept payment in kind, which took many forms, from fresh eggs to treasured possessions, which no doubt would become valuable antiques, years down the line. This practice would end in 1948.

Never Had It So Good.

During the fifties, the N.H.S. struggled to keep pace with the demands placed upon it. People had struggled with non life threatening, treatable conditions for many years, because they hadn't the ability to pay. Suddenly, treatment became available to all and everybody joined the queue. This was one of the reasons why the service expanded very rapidly, and this country, didn't have the man power with the necessary expertise to fully staff it. Doctors were in great demand and were imported, mostly from India. An obvious choice, since India had been under British rule until 1947. Most of their medical schools were aligned to the British standard and were over seen by the General Medical Council. The first language in the Indian higher education establishments was English, another bonus. Girls were recruited from Ireland and the West Indies to do nurse training. The famous or infamous, whichever way you look at it M.P. Enoch Powell, was minister of health during this time, and was personally responsible for this recruitment, visiting higher secondary schools in these countries, espousing the benefits of relocating to Great Britain. Having spent many years working with these people, I can say that they were most hard working and conscientious, in fact, everyone in the health service had a dedication to the job second to none.

Never Had It So Good.

Hospitals were run like clockwork, the Matron and a senior medical consultant, along with a small lay board, managed the whole establishment. Cleanliness was essential; sinks were cleaned on a daily basis, a good scrub down with Vim, until they shone, along with the plug and chain which had to be cleaned at the same time. Early morning duties involved cleaning the sterilising room, trolleys were turned upside down, in order to clean and oil the wheels. All the instruments would be placed in the huge stainless steel sterilizer and boiled, the water being changed daily. All the sterilising was done on the wards, and the trolleys were laid, with the necessary instruments before the dressing rounds began. On the opposite side of the ward was the sluice, the dirty room, kept well away from the sterilizing room for obvious reasons. This room had to be scrubbed clean too along with all the bedpans which were stainless steel. These were scrubbed with Jeyes fluid, a powerful disinfectant which pervaded the whole of the hospital, and gave rise to the description, the hospital smell. Sputum pots were emptied and washed, after the contents had been measured and recorded, not everybody's favourite job. While some staff, usually the juniors, were assigned work in the sluice and sterilizing rooms, others were busy bed making, top sheet to the bottom, and clean sheet on the top every day. Bed bound patients were bed bathed at the same time and ambulant patients taken to the bath rooms. All this was completed by about 9am when, by rota we would go to "dress". This was a 30 minute break, during which time we had a cup of tea or coffee, slice of toast and then changed into beautifully laundered starched white aprons etc. On return to the wards, the clean work would begin. Medicines and injections were administered and on surgical wards dressings would be changed. Consultants would do rounds, junior doctors did daily visits. Patients were ferried back and forth to theatre, x-ray, physio and other departments. New patients admitted and old ones discharged, at which point, the bed, locker and everything else was thoroughly disinfected. At some point during these very busy days, the food wagon, a stainless steel heated container would arrive from the kitchens. The ward sister or staff nurse in charge, served up the meals. Every member of staff lined up with a tray and would be told which patient a certain meal was intended for. Certain members of staff were assigned to feeding duties and there seemed to be a lot of patients who were unable to feed themselves. Treatments were vastly different then. Anyone admitted with a heart attack, lay flat on their backs for six weeks, were bed bathed and fed the whole time. Cataract surgery rendered a patient unable to lift their heads more than a couple of inches for about ten days, now they leave hospital within a couple of hours.

Never Had It So Good.

Visiting was for thirty minutes on five evenings a week, and for one hour on two afternoons, usually Thursday, being the local half day closing and Sunday. Only two visitors were allowed at any one time. On children's ward, visitors were allowed only on the two afternoons. It must have been dreadful for those poor mites, deprived of their mothers when they most needed them. The psychological needs of patients, especially children, wasn't understood until some years later when mother care units started to open, which allowed a mother or carer to stay whole time.

Apart from the daily clean, a super mega clean took place took place on two afternoons a week. Day one, all the beds, lockers and chairs etc, were dragged from one side of the ward to the centre. The backs of all the beds and furniture were cleaned. The walls and windows were high dusted. The central heating pipes running along the walls and skirting boards were cleaned, followed by the floors. These were usually wooden block. They were washed with a special soapy solution and dried. Polish was applied and this was buffed up using a huge wooden block on the end of a long handle. It was pushed back and forth time and again until the floor had been covered from end to end. The beds and furniture was then returned to its normal position. Day two usually the following afternoon, saw the same process repeated on the other side of the ward. Every member of staff was involved in this procedure, from the ward sister down to the cleaner, in those days called a domestic. We were part of a team and we worked as a team. If a job needed doing it got done, it wasn't passed around and everybody had a pride in their work.

In spite of the hardship and suffering, experienced by the majority of the population, before the inception of the N.H.S., many weren't satisfied. Free treatment, glasses, dentures, corsets etc wasn't enough. It was well known for people to have three of everything, one for work, one for weekend and one spare. Abuse of the system became rife, there is a saying, if you don't pay for it, you don't appreciate it, and in many ways it's true. It wasn't long before the N.H.S. bill was becoming far more expensive than ever envisaged.

In most cases the change in fortune was for the better, but life in many respects remained quite primitive. We still had outside toilets, though the newspaper had been replaced by proper toilet paper, a brand called Izal was the one I remember, it was not quilted and soft as now.

However, things were looking up, and the idea of space exploration had been conceived. It was about to be born with the launch of the first spacecraft. It was Russian and was called the Sputnik. It was launched unmanned, into the unknown in 1957. As darkness fell, we searched the skies, terrified. Rumours were rife, it was heading for the moon, nobody knew what the moon consisted of, and the general theory, was that it was a ball of gas. Once hit, it would explode and that would be the end of us all. Not to be, it didn't hit the moon and we all lived to enjoy the swinging sixties.

THE SWINGING SIXTIES AND BEYOND.

To have arrived at this point, following three, even four decades of hardship and two world wars, is a testament to the tenacity and power of the human spirit. The doom and gloom mongers had been proved wrong. The bad old days of hardship and war, struggle and strife were well and truly in the past. A new era had dawned; it could have been another world. The biggest changes, affecting all aspects of our moral and social history were about to happen.

Full employment gave us the readies which, in turn gave us choice and freedom. The government had a fair amount in their coffers too, and this afforded noticeable improvements in health, education and transport.

New hospitals now replaced many Victorian buildings. Medical techniques became vastly improved; the first heart transplant was performed, followed in time by the transplantation of many other organs. It became possible to replace worn out joints, a symptom associated with our longer life span. Home births were reduced as maternity beds increased, cutting the risk of infant and maternal mortality. State of the art, special care baby units saved the lives of the tiniest babies.

A revolution in education was about to unfold, GCE "O" and "A" level were now commonplace. Junior school became a middle school. The secondary moderns and in some authorities, the high and grammar schools were amalgamated into mixed ability comprehensives. The authorities at the time, believed this system to be fair to all. To accommodate this new idea, huge school buildings were erected, in order to house as many as one thousand pupils at any one time. Whether this was a good or bad idea, depended then as now, on your point of view or the colour of your political party. Some authorities retained the eleven plus exam and the grammar and high schools that still exist are doing well.

The transport network of motorways and dual carriageways, gained pace as the decade unfolded, cars were becoming more affordable as they were mass produced and wages increased. One of the cheapest and most popular was the mini, designed by Sir Alex Isigonis and produced by British Leyland. In the early sixties, even I owned a car, albeit an Austin A30, commonly known as a baby Austin. It was my pride and joy, in spite of it being a bit of a banger. The radiator must have had a serious leak, because I remember putting more Radweld in the radiator than petrol in the tank. It probably cost more than the petrol, which from memory was about four shillings a gallon in old money, equivalent to twenty pence today. The need for personal transport increased tremendously, as families migrated in search of better housing or work, and because, shopping patterns changed as huge out of town shopping malls were created, in the last couple of decades.

Home ownership wasn't just for the rich and famous anymore, it now extended to the working classes. There was a proliferation of Building Societies, whose specific purpose at the time, was to lend money in the form of mortgages for house purchase. The rules for borrowing were very strict and certain criteria had to be fulfilled before any loan was agreed. Living standards rapidly started to improve, to the extent that the very cold winter of 1963, didn't see the slag heaps covered in humanity, every body could afford the extra coal necessary to keep the cold at bay. Ariel's could be seen sprouting from every chimney, as televisions became available to the majority. The programmes were limited to a few hours a day, and in the very early days was only BBC. The universal favourite was Val Parnell's, Sunday night at the London Palladium. Children's programmes were just one half hour a day and were either, Muffin the Mule or Bill and Ben the flower pot men. The news was always preceded by a picture of a transmitter. In between the programmes were interludes, when a picture was shown; one of the favourites was of a potter at his wheel. Some people with nothing better to do, kept the

The Swinging Sixties And Beyond.

television on, programme or not, until the national anthem came on, it wasn't unknown for people to stand for this. Only when the white spot appeared was it turned off.

The kitchens became fitted; these varied from the basic to the extremely complicated, even having work stations in the centre if space allowed. Fitted washing machines, fridges and dishwashers became common place. Many would not have looked out of place in a stately home. Bathrooms also took on a new look, they started to be sited up stairs, much more convenient, a definite improvement on being next to the kitchen. Coloured suites which consisted of bath, wash hand basin and low coupled toilets were the norm. Gold plated fittings were available for the very ostentatious. The walls were invariably tiled, at least half way, but sometimes floor to ceiling. In newer build houses, en-suite facilities, usually shower, toilet and hand basin, were included even in the smallest of properties, in effect providing two bathrooms, a far cry from the kitchen sink.

Home furnishings and decoration started to take on a very different role, from necessity to must have. Leather replaced the Rexine, occasional tables, of all shapes and sizes had a place in every living room, which by now had become a lounge. Plastic flowers were dumped in favour of more exotic silk flowers. The lino and bare floor boards were replaced with wall to wall carpet, when this first happened, neighbours could be heard to say, "they've gone all bay windowed" in other words posh. Fashions in soft furnishings, changed quite a number of times from plain and simple lines to the very decorative swags and tails, the quality, and design varied according to the purse, in some cases were very regal and elegant. To accommodate these changes a new industry was born, it was called interior design. This affluence wasn't limited to the lounge, it extended to the bedrooms. Whole houses were given a make over and that included the gardens. Furniture changed too, the big, bulky, solid wooden tables and sideboards went on the bonfire and were replaced by lighter stuff, more modern as in G Plan, or reproduction regency type.

During the seventies and eighties people started to socialise, up until this time, the lads met in the pub and the women had a coffee, very few pubs at that time served food. Home entertaining took off in a big way; housewives vied for the position of the hostess with the mostess, doing the rounds and being on the social calendar meant that you'd made it. Crystal glasses and matching china dinner services, manufactured by the best potters of course, were on display, these were in great demand and saw the potters in full production. The other must have items were the drinks cabinet, containing a variety of wines and spirits; it wouldn't do, not to offer a big choice. The soda stream and coffee percolator were well used. Possibly the most important and very convenient item, was the hostess trolley, it made entertaining much easier. Food could be prepared earlier, allowing the hostess the time to scrub up before the guests arrived. In the seventies, it was customary for gentlemen always to wear lounge suits, and ladies long dresses. Two decades later, more casual attire was adopted and house parties had a slow death, as pubs started to serve a limited menu of inexpensive bar food, chicken nuggets in a basket being one of the favourites.

Around the sixties saw the birth of the teenager, until this time children evolved into adults over night, the in between years didn't exist. It had been school and part time jobs for most, school and homework for those considered brighter and capable of higher education. At the age of fifteen, it was full time work, a time of earning your keep and paying your dues, time for accountability and responsibility. It became a case of let the good times roll and they certainly did. A new generation evolved, flower power, love all thy neighbours and every body else, behavioural boundaries changed, the hippy had arrived, many of these young people decided to drop out of society, to facilitate this, they set up communes.

The Swinging Sixties And Beyond.

The birth control pill was introduced in the sixties, it was intended to allow women the opportunity to plan pregnancies and in effect take control of their lives, it did far more than that. Fear was removed and sexual freedom was the result. For some sex became more adventurous, this was the start of the sex revolution, a new activity evolved called wife swapping, usually performed in private. Towards the end of the century this had become big business and became known as swinging, no longer private but performed in clubs and involving huge numbers of people. The Abortion act was passed in 1968, legalising abortion. This procedure had always been performed, albeit by the back door, known as back street abortions. These were often performed by unscrupulous people, in unsterile conditions, resulting in sepsis, injury and even death. Moves were afoot to end the stigma of homosexuality, this resulted in the condition being decriminalised in the 1980's.

Music started to play a big part especially in the lives of the young. The birth of rock and roll brought with it pop groups such as the Beetles, Bill Haley and the comets, Cliff Richard and the Shadows and singers such as Cilla Black and Sandy Shaw. Programmes such as Top of the Pops appealed to a certain age group, and had an enormous following. Pop concerts and music festivals became part of the scene and have retained a massive

The Swinging Sixties And Beyond.

following for decades. Anything to do with music was in vogue, record players, tape recorders and transistors. Seventy eight inch vinyl records were replaced by a smaller version, much later to be replaced by C.D.'s.

The bigger version of the vinyls, eventually being made into plant pots. This was done by placing the record in very hot water, when pliable it was moulded into the desired shape, a use was found for everything. Divisions among young people were created, by a leaning towards one type of music as opposed to another. The Teddy Boys were a good example, easily recognisable by their drain pipe trousers, crepe soled, suede shoes, long black jackets with a red or purple lining and lapels, and the boot lace tie. The hair, heavily Brylcreemed was combed straight back, a trade mark quaff or kiss curl hung over the fore head. There were the Mods and the Rockers, mostly young men with a penchant for the motor scooter. Either the Vespa or the Lambretta according to whether you were a mod or a rocker. These groups were fine as long as they were apart, trouble could be expected, and a scuffle was on the cards if they met up, not always by accident. Trouble only flared between groups, it was rarely directed towards an individual.

Fashions changed virtually every month; from the very elegant to the very casual, everything could be in fashion at the same time, and often followed whatever was in vogue with a particular celebrity. Skirt lengths went from, mini to midi to maxi; pencil tight, straight skirts to full circular skirts, floral and plain. Trousers were either very tight or flared, with or without turn ups, shirt collars were very big or very small, and ties were very thick or very thin. Shoes went from very pointed winkle pickers to square toes, stiletto heels to wedges, a lot of these styles, were not only applicable to shoes for the fairer sex. Jeans were invented, and have been the one fashion item, that has remained unchanged for decades. Trousers became a popular item in the female wardrobe, an item of clothing universal for all ages. Fur coats, hats and stoles had at one time been worn by the better off, a fashion statement if you like, this was one thing that didn't survive the end of the century, animal welfare activists put paid to that.

There was much to celebrate in the sixties, if the fifties was the decade when we had never had it so good, then the sixties was the decade when it could only get better. In 1966 during a glorious summer, under the leadership of Alf Ramsey, England won the world cup, the country was ecstatic. Manned space flights followed the sputnik; the Russians were again in the lead, with Yuri Gagarin being the first man in space. The Americans were not best pleased, and their then president J.F.Kennedy, promised that the Americans would be the first, to send a manned craft to the moon. They had obviously established that it was a solid object, and a successful mission was accomplished in 1968. The same year, saw the birth of the first successful test tube baby, a world first, engineered in England.

The world suddenly became a much smaller place, holidays moved on from Butlins and the Costa Brava; long haul flights gave access to far flung exotic destinations. Our knowledge of other countries, their people, culture, food and religion increased. The media including television gave these people an insight into life in the industrialised world. Full employment saw an influx of foreign workers, arriving here to fill unskilled, low paid jobs mainly on production lines especially in the car industry. During the last couple of decades of the twentieth century, demand was high. Production was at full pelt day and night to satisfy the demand. Immigration to this country from all corners of the world, continued apace throughout this time. It would produce a culturally diverse country, in many ways it enriched our society, we had an understanding of other races. Great Britain had previously governed most of these countries for a number of centuries, and for some reason operated an open door policy, allowing entry to ever increasing numbers. Whether this was good or bad, only history will tell.

The Swinging Sixties And Beyond.

Throughout our history there had been highs and lows in our national and individual prosperity. The seventies saw just such a low, an economic recession, this was brought about by job losses in our manufacturing industries. The country was put on a three day a week; this caused massive disruption, power cuts affected the whole country. On a domestic level we had power cuts on a rota basis which enabled some advance preparation. Water was boiled and kept in thermos flasks, hot water bottles were filled which helped stave off the cold when central heating failed and electric fires and cookers were of no use. Candles replaced lights, televisions were blank and silent. The shops ran out of candles and calor gas heaters and hobs were in great demand, even small primus stoves were put to very good use. Debts could not be paid and neither could mortgages, so, houses were put on the market, in some cases as repossessions by the mortgage lender. This caused a slump in house prices but, as is usual once the job market and the financial situation stabilised, house values recovered.

The unions had long fought for better working conditions; employers saw this a little differently in some cases as interference. Time and motion studies became part and parcel of assessing time management, not only on the shop floor, but also at the desk. Over a period of time, automation had been creeping into the

The Swinging Sixties And Beyond.

work place, to buck this trend, strikes again became the weapon of the work force.

The eighties saw the unions in direct opposition to the government. Strikes, starting with the miners were widespread and were fuelled by the use of flying pickets. Another recession loomed, so did a prolonged period of hardship, families were divided as fathers, sons and brothers with opposing views, were pitted against each other creating a bitterness, that in some cases, even time could not heal. The country was brought to its knees, the Prime Minister, Margaret Thatcher stood her ground, laws were passed to restrict union powers and to ban flying pickets. It seemed that in no time at all, most of the pits closed in spite of a hard fought battle to keep them open. This battle was soon extended to other industries especially steel. Power stations started to import coal from Eastern Europe and Asia.

A pattern seemed to be developing as another recession was on the cards. This time it was the early nineties, with it came a loss in individual and national prosperity. Fewer people in work meant a loss of income for the government in taxes and national insurance, there is also an increase in government expenses, owing to the payment of unemployment and social security benefits. The government coffers started to decline, a situation that was rectified by privatising the nationalised utilities as in gas, telephone, electricity and rail. Most of us were given a few shares before these companies were floated on the stock market, some made a handsome profit in a very short time. Within a decade or so, many of these companies were owned by foreign companies, much of our gas would eventually come from Russia, our government had no control or say in how much we would have to pay for commodities so necessary for our survival and economic growth. Building societies, which had previously belonged to members, i.e. people with either savings or mortgages, decided to become banks, which had always operated with less restricted practices.

With the coffers replenished, things were on the up again, and we were on a roll. Unemployment started to decline, but jobs were in a very different type of employment. Many of our manufacturing jobs and skills had been lost for good. The pits had all closed, the other major employer, the pottery manufacturers were struggling to survive. The answer seemed to be amalgamation of factories, this pattern continued until a couple of groups owned all the major names. Labour costs were cheaper abroad, a new word entered the dictionary, it was outsourcing, jobs went abroad, a practice that was not confined to the pottery industry.

The Swinging Sixties And Beyond.

Jobs were created in information technology or I.T. which had taken off in a big way. Tiny electrical components called chips became part of everyday life. We had mobile 'phones, personal C.D. and D.V.D. players along with satellite television. Jobs were also created in the service industries, hotels became affordable and popular for weekends and short breaks, people wanted more luxury than the older bed and breakfast boarding houses provided. Pubs started to serve bar meals and restaurant food, restaurants became prolific across towns and cities offering any amount of English and ethnic dishes, foreign travel and our culturally diverse society had changed the British pallet, which craved spicy exotic fare. As eating out became the norm, home entertaining declined, bringing with it a devaluation of the dinner services, so prized just a decade before.

Leisure, a word unknown a few decades earlier, became an industry. Leisure clubs and gyms opened up on a small scale at first in hotels, for the use of residents and members. As demand for these services grew, the industry became bigger and better with sports arenas and big fitness centres providing multiple disciplines, from basic aerobics to pilates and yoga. Spa centres arrived on the scene, providing luxury treatments and relaxation.

The Swinging Sixties And Beyond.

It seemed like we had at last reached nirvana.
Working hours were reduced; we had more free
time, and money by the bucketful.
Unfortunately, choice, freedom and prosperity,
doesn't necessarily equate to wisdom. Drugs of
all descriptions had been introduced in the
seventies and eighties. By the nineties the use
of certain drugs almost equalled that of
tobacco. Drug money was a big earner and was
thought to be funding terrorism, which,
although around for generations, was
becoming more sophisticated, another phrase
added to our language was money laundering,
which was associated with these and other
activities. The downside to the drug industry is
well documented, and is addiction, a state that
can reduce a decent human being, to a
destitute wreck, bringing untold misery to
families and the wider community.
Unfortunately this sometimes involves our
children, who can be introduced to these
substances at the school gates.

Towards the end of the century, a noticeable
change had taken place, a situation that had
been evolving slowly and quietly over a number
of years, the demise of the community. The
glue that had kept us together through thick
and thin, in bad times and good, had gone. It
had become a society apart; neighbours didn't
even know each others names. It was
everyman for himself; the I'm alright jack
attitude and it extended from the very top to

the bottom of our society. However, the good times were still good, the British entrepreneurial skills created more millionaires, and the working classes had more disposable income than ever before.

A new millennium was fast approaching; the better times could only get better. A new beginning caused excitement and expectation in every household, city and country across the world.

FULL CIRCLE.

The fireworks that heralded this momentous occasion bore no resemblance to the small box of assorted fireworks, that we had shared six decades earlier. Television allowed us to watch the spectacle from around the world, as this occasion was celebrated at different times in countries from east to west, all hoping to outdo every body else by a bigger and better display. A competitiveness that extended to the individual, money was no object, we enjoyed an affluence that would have been hard to imagine possible, just half a century ago. The millennium brought with it some fears, the main one was that all computers would crash, due to a millennium bug, a fear that proved to be unfounded, a bit like the Sputnik. Information Technology, I.T. for short, had started to dominate our lives, from supermarket bar codes to a national computer data base, every man, woman and child was included, the information held, covered all aspects of our lives, big brother had at last arrived.

Everything was available and we all had to have a slice of the cake. Property prices went through the roof, as we aspired to bigger and better. The construction industry was booming as house building soared to meet demand. Land prices were at a premium, even back gardens were sold to developers, the not in my back yard attitude went through the window.

Full Circle.

TV's became smart slim line flat screen sets, their size and position, along with other accoutrements such as the Digibox, Video and D.V.D. players, conveyed their importance in home entertainment. Wooden or laminate flooring started to replace the wall to wall carpets that had once been a measure of success. Traditional pictures were replaced with simple modern designs. Royal Doulton ladies and other ornaments so favoured in the past were moth balled. Everything had to match; minimalism became the new word as simple, sleeker lines were in vogue. A home study became a requirement to house such necessities as the computer, which allowed wonderful internet access. Specially designed desks housed scanners, copiers and laminators. Many executives now spend much of their time working from home, modern 'phones facilitating conference calling, allowing contact with more than one colleague at a time. Not everything got bigger, many things got much smaller, mobile 'phones which combined camera and video, would fit in the palm of the hand, as would digital cameras, we had come a long way from the box Brownie camera that we had all been so proud to own. Personal C.D. players, which were the must have a decade ago, have now been replaced by M.P.3 players, which are about the size of a fifty pence piece and contain a huge amount of memory. Paper road maps are gradually being

Full Circle.

replaced by the in car Sat Nav, just type in the post code, follow the verbal instructions, and arrival at your destination is a certainty. Some vehicles have found themselves up the creek, so it isn't an exact science yet. Fashions also changed and a designer label was as important as the item itself, which included shoes, trainers, belts, handbags and virtually every thing else. The down side was that the children of families unable to pay exorbitant prices for these items were in danger of being bullied by their peers.

Terrorism reared its ugly head in 2001, When the Twin Towers in New York were brought down using air planes. This single act, elicited a swift response from the west, and the so called war on terror began. This saw the U.S.A., Great Britain and other allies engaged in war on two fronts, Afghanistan and Iraq, operations continues almost a decade later. There was much public opposition to this response; many took to the streets in cities up and down the country, but especially in the capital. This opposition has remained constant, many believing war to be destructive, too many innocents suffer needlessly. The bullet solves nothing and may even serve to increase division, dialogue should never be exhausted.

This act of terrorism suggested a sinister, underlying rage, casting doubt over our individual and national security. Civil liberties became questionable, and more than ever before surveillance played a big part in our lives. This was made possible by C.C.T.V. in shops, town centres and on our roads. It is estimated, that an individual going about their normal business, can be photographed over one hundred and fifty times a day. Mobile 'phone calls and internet access can be monitored and information stored, to be retrieved in the future if required. Identity cards have been the subject of debate for a number of years; I have no problem with the idea, especially if they contain biometric features, which is now possible. The lobby against, believe them to be an erosion of our liberty, is that already lost?

There have been changes to the national facilities that we have come to take for granted, the National Health Service is a case in point. Treatment for some conditions, though available is no longer guaranteed. Changes to our life style and increased longevity, has seen a rise in the prevalence of certain illnesses. Drugs exist to treat many conditions including certain cancers, and devastating types of dementia as in Alzheimer's. Unfortunately, a cap on local N.H.S. budgets, prevents certain prescribing, some areas fare better than others, a situation, that has become universally known as post code lottery. Are we reaching a point, when free treatment ceases,

Full Circle.

as in the pre 1948 era? Free dental treatment was abolished many years ago; patients were expected to pay a percentage of the treatment cost. Now, patients are hard pressed to find an N.H.S. dentist at all, and in some cases the treatment offered is quite inferior to that available a number of years ago. Free eye tests, except for a few have also been abolished.

Respect for law and order has totally changed. No longer is an elderly or infirm person sure of a seat on a bus. Damage to property seems to be a national sport. Gun and knife crime is out of control. The only police on the streets now, seem to be volunteer special constables, hardened trouble makers challenging their authority. A far cry from the local bobby, who knew who we were and where we lived, there was no point in dropping the spoils of our scrumping and running, we got taken home, where punishment was duly delivered and a lesson learned.

A phrase never heard before was on every ones lips, it was the credit crunch. It suddenly dawned, that the fantastic, extravagant life style that we had all become accustomed to, had been funded by borrowing, a new sickness prevailed, it was called Afluenza, which was a financial cold. It is estimated that individual debt in Great Britain equalled approximately £30,000 for every head of population. The national purse was low on funds too, it was

Full Circle.

replenished when the chancellor sold a good proportion of our gold, with hindsight this proved to have been a bad idea. At the time of selling gold prices were low, but within a short time were to rise enormously.

Credit to businesses and individuals has dried up, with devastating consequences. On an individual level, belts have been tightened and spending reigned in as credit has been harder to find. Town centres, which had been in decline for some time due to the popularity of out of town shopping, now show the signs of terminal illness, as shop after shop goes into administration, including the likes of Woolworths, with a ninety nine year trading history. Pubs are reckoned to be closing at the rate of five a week, as people have started drinking at home, a wide selection of alcohol available on the super market shelves. Is home entertaining about to make a come back, are the prized dinner services about to regain their value, will a place in the dining room be found for the hostess trolley, and should we all have held on to the soda stream? More people have taken to growing their own vegetables, and there are now queues for council allotments. The rag and bone man has made a return; the horse has been retired, in favour of a motorised pick up.

Within a decade of this wonderful new beginning, the biggest catastrophe for almost a

Full Circle.

century was about to unfold. The banks were going to the wall, queues formed as depositors rushed to draw out their life savings. The government came to the rescue, with massive loans, leading to part nationalisation. The big one was about to happen, the past was about to make an appearance, Wall Street crashed.

Panic spread through the world markets as the global financial institutions reported big problems. Money was no longer available as banks reported their own massive debts. Industry was left struggling big time, and the lack of credit saw many go into administration of one form or another. Wedgwood, a china factory in production for two hundred and fifty years, during which time, it had survived a number of recessions and down turns, didn't escape unscathed. This situation affected manufacturers, big and small across this land, creating a rise in unemployment not seen for many a decade a situation that brings with it, untold misery for many, and a change to our social fabric. House values have crashed as prices plummet, due to repossessions or lack of available mortgages for people still in a position to buy.

This situation has been brought about in part by greed and the irresponsibility of bankers. Too many risky deals have been taken and they have ended up with burnt fingers. Unfortunately we have all ended up in the fire, but have we come full circle?

EPILOGUE.

This is a true recollection of the past sixty to seventy years or so. Not every situation described applies to me personally or domestically. They are however, a record of events witnessed by me both as a child and in my nursing and midwifery career.

My grandchildren, all under twelve years, would not recognise the life of ordinary working class people, just a couple of generations ago.

It was my intention, to give them and their peers, an insight into the past, to help them appreciate the privileges they now enjoy, to have an understanding of the many less fortunate, and to realise, that not all things are permanent. I hope I have succeeded.

This is a recollection, of the lives of the working class population about sixty to seventy years ago. The situations and conditions described were in the Stoke-on-Trent area, but would apply to any industrial town or city in Great Britain.